MESSIANIC PROPHECIES

IN

HISTORICAL SUCCESSION.

MESSIANIC PROPHECIES

IN

HISTORICAL SUCCESSION.

BY

FRANZ DELITZSCH.

TRANSLATED BY

SAMUEL IVES CURTISS,
PROFESSOR IN CHICAGO THEOLOGICAL SEMINARY.

Wipf and Stock Publishers
150 West Broadway • Eugene OR 97401

Messianic Prophecies in Historical Succession
by Franz Delitzsch

ISBN: 1-57910-077-5

Printed by  1998

TO

THE MEMORY OF

MY BELOVED AND ONLY DAUGHTER

PAULINE,

WHO ENTERED INTO REST

THREE DAYS AFTER THE DEPARTURE OF

MY REVERED FRIEND AND TEACHER

PROF. FRANZ DELITZSCH, D.D.

TRANSLATOR'S PREFACE.

———o———

This little volume is a fitting crown to the exegetical studies of Dr. Delitzsch. From various points of view it is likely to be of unusual interest, not only to those who have been accustomed to peruse his works, but also to others.

The proofs of the original were read by the lamented author as he was confined to his bed by his last illness, weak in body, but clear in mind. The preface which he dictated five days before his departure was his final literary work. The last printed sheet was laid on his bed the day before he died.

Already the orginal has received high praise from appreciative scholars. It is hoped that the translation may be found not unworthy of this legacy to the cause of Jewish missions by a revered teacher and friend.

SAMUEL IVES CURTISS.

Chicago, *Feb. 2nd*, 1891.

AUTHOR'S PREFACE.

---o---

As in the summer of 1887 I delivered my Lectures on the Messianic Prophecies, perhaps for the last time, as I had reason to believe, I sought to put the product of my long scientific investigation into as brief, attractive, and suggestive a form as possible. At the same time the wish inspired me to leave as a legacy: to the *Institutum Judaicum* the compendium of a *Concordia fidei* ; to our missionaries a *Vade mecum*.

Thus arose this little book—a late sheaf from old and new grain. May God own the old as not obsolete, the new as not obsolescent!

FRANZ DELITZSCH.

LEIPZIG, *Feb.* 26, 1890.

CONTENTS.

---o---

PRELIMINARY REMARKS.

INTRODUCTION.

SECT.		PAGE
1.	The Twofold Character of the Problem expressed by the Name,	9
2.	The Historical Significance of that which is apparently isolated,	10
3.	The Indispensableness of Literary and Historical Criticism,	12
4.	The Reasonableness of the Supernatural,	12
5.	The Redemption a Logical Necessity,	14
6.	Messianic Prophecy with and without mention of the Messiah,	15
7.	Messianic Prophecies in the Narrowest Signification,	16
8.	The New Testament Glorification of the Conception of the Messiah,	18
9.	Messianic Prophecies in a Broader Signification,	21
10.	Historical Sketch of the Subject,	22

MESSIANIC PROPHECIES IN HISTORICAL SUCCESSION.

CHAPTER I.

THE DIVINE WORD CONCERNING THE FUTURE SALVATION BEFORE THE TIME OF THE PROPHETS.

1.	Justification of the Beginning in Gen. iii.,	31
2.	Beginning and Object of the Theophanies,	33
3.	The Primitive Promise,	34
4.	The Primitive Promise in the Light of Fulfilment,	36

x CONTENTS.

SECT.	PAGE
5. Finest Effects and Verifications of the Primitive Promise,	39
6. The Expected Comforter,	42
7. The Promise of the Blessing of the Nations in the Seed of the Patriarchs,	43

CHAPTER II.

THE PROPHETIC BENEDICTIONS OF THE DYING PATRIARCHS.

8. Jacob's artful Procurement of the Blessing of the First-Born,	47
9. The Designation of Judah as the Royal and Messianic Tribe,	50

CHAPTER III.

THE PREDICTIONS OF THE MOSAIC PERIOD CONCERNING THE FUTURE SALVATION.

10. The Promise of a Prophet after Moses, and like him,	59
11. The Prophecy of Balaam concerning the Star and the Sceptre out of Israel,	65
12. Course and Goal of the History of Salvation after Moses' great Memorial Song,	69

CHAPTER IV.

THE MESSIANIC PROPHECIES OF THE TIME OF JOSHUA AND OF THE JUDGES.

13. Yahweh and His Anointed in the Thanksgiving Song of Hannah,	74
14. The divinely-anointed One in the Threatening Prophecy concerning the House of Eli,	76

CHAPTER V.

PROPHECY AND CHOKMA IN THE AGE OF DAVID AND SOLOMON.

15. The Transition of the Kingdom from Benjamin to Judah,	80
16. David's View of Himself after his anointing,	82

CONTENTS. xi

SECT.		PAGE
17.	The Binding of the Promise to the House of David,	85
18.	The Separation of the Image of the Messiah from the Person of David,	89
19.	David's Testamentary Words,	94
20.	Messianic Desires and Hopes of Solomon,	97
21.	Prophecy and Chokma,	99
22.	The Goël and the Mediating Angel in the Book of Job,	102

CHAPTER VI.

PROPHECY AND CHOKMA IN THE FIRST EPOCHS OF THE DIVISION OF THE KINGDOM.

23.	The Prophets after the Division of the Kingdom until the Reign of Jehoshaphat and the Dynasty of Omri,	106
24.	The Metaphysical Conception of Wisdom in the Introduction to the Book of Proverbs,	108
25.	The Epithalamium, Ps. xlv.,	112

CHAPTER VII.

THE MESSIANIC ELEMENTS IN THE PROPHETIC LITERATURE FROM JORAM TO HEZEKIAH.

26.	The Relation of the three oldest Prophetic Writings to the Messianic Idea,	116
27.	The View of Hosea, the Ephraimitic Prophet of the Final Period,	126
28.	Isaiah's Fundamental Ideas in their Original Form,	135
29.	The Great Trilogy of Messianic Prophecies, Isa, vii., ix., xi.,	138
	I. Immanuel, the Son of the Virgin,	138
30.	The Great Trilogy of Messianic Prophecies, Isa. vii., ix., xi.,	143
	II. The Beginning of a new Period with the new Heir of the Davidic Throne,	143
31.	The Great Trilogy of Messianic Prophecies, Isa. vii., ix., xi.,	147
	III. Characteristics of the Second David and of his Government,	147
32.	The Son of God in Psalm ii.,	152
33.	The Messianic Elements in the Addresses of Isaiah, xiv. 24–xxxix.,	156
34.	The Elements of Progress in Micah's Messianic Proclamation,	160

CHAPTER VIII.

PROPHECY FROM THE TIME OF HEZEKIAH UNTIL THE CATASTROPHE.

SECT.	PAGE
35. The Domain of Nahum's and Zephaniah's Vision,	168
36. Habakkuk's Solution of Faith, and Faith's Object,	171
37. Mediately Messianic Elements in Jeremiah's Announcement until the carrying away of Jehoiachin,	176
38. Immediate Messianic Elements in Jeremiah's Prophecies under Zedekiah until after the Destruction of Jerusalem,	180

CHAPTER IX.

PROPHECY IN THE BABYLONIAN EXILE.

39. The Messiah in Ezekiel,	188
40. The Prince in Ezekiel's Future State,	193
41. The Metamorphosis of the Messianic Ideal in Isa. xl.–lxvi.,	197
42. The Servant of Yahweh in Deutero-Isaiah,	201
43. The Mediator of Salvation as Prophet, Priest, and King in one Person,	203
44. The Great Finale, Isa. xxiv.–xxvii.,	206

CHAPTER X.

THE PROPHECY OF THE PERIOD OF THE RESTORATION.

45. Post-Exilic Prophecy in view of the New Temple,	210
46. The Two Christological Pairs of Prophecy in Deutero-Zechariah,	214
I. The First Prophetic Pair in Chaps. ix.–xi.,	214
47. The Two Christological Pairs of Prophecy in Deutero-Zechariah,	219
II. The Second Prophetic Pair in Chaps. xii.–xiv.,	219
48. Concluding Prophecies of New Testament Contents in Malachi,	223
49. The Antichrist in the Book of Daniel,	228
50. Christ in the Book of Daniel,	230

PRELIMINARY REMARKS.

---o---

IT is undeniable, and is universally recognised, that in the Scriptures of the Old Testament, One divinely anointed, a Messiah, who is to go forth from Israel, is promised and hoped for, who makes His people victorious and powerful, and who from them extends His dominion to a world dominion. The Jews still look for this Messiah; Christianity—and to a certain extent also Islam—sees the promise fulfilled in Jesus. This Jesus is regarded by us Christians as the promised Christ, *i.e.* the Messiah.[1] Christianity is the

[1] Sadly morbid exceptions to this Christian recognition of Jesus as the Christ are made in Konynenburg's investigations concerning the nature of the Old Testament prophecies respecting the Messiah, who entirely denies the existence of Messianic prophecies, which have been fulfilled, or are to be fulfilled,[1] since he considers the expectation which the Jews entertain of an ideal King as a product of moral perversity : also by Lord Amberly, who declares that the rejection of Jesus as Messiah is fully justifiable, since it is an astonishing assumption on the part of Gentile Christians, that they are more competent than the Jews themselves to give an opinion, as to what the name of the Messiah signifies and requires.[2]

---

[1] Konynenburg, *Untersuchung über die Natur der Alttestamentl. Weissagungen auf den Messias aus dem Holländischen übersetzt*, Lugen 1759, 395 ff.

[2] *An Analysis of Religious Belief*, London 1876, vol. i. p. 388 f.

same as the religion of the Messiah, the religion which has the Christ, who appeared in Jesus, as its principle and centre.

Hence the name Christianity indicates that it claims to be the religion which is being prepared in the history and word and writing of the Old Testament. Even when we call it the New Testament religion, we thus recognise that it is the religion of a covenant which has taken the place of the old, but not without having the old as a first step, and not without standing in connection with it as the fruit with the tree, the child with the mother.

Hence Christianity in the Old Testament is in the process of development. With the same propriety we can say: Christ, through the Old Testament, is in the act of coming. Is is true that the man Jesus has a temporal beginning, beyond which His existence as a man does not extend. But in this fact, that He appeared in the fulness of time, God's counsel was fulfilled; and since Jesus is certainly the man who above all others had God dwelling in Himself, the approach of God, who proposes to reveal Himself and perfect the work of salvation through Him, is at the same time an approach of Jesus. His coming in the Old Testament is therefore something more than merely ideal.

These are views which Christians hold in common —indisputable propositions which, from a Christian standpoint, express a historical fact without presupposing any closer dogmatic statements. We emphasize this intentionally, in order to attract as far as possible the circle of those to whose sympathy we appeal for the following investigations. How much we should rejoice, if we could also secure the sympathy of those belonging to the Jewish confession who are seeking after the truth. It is indeed worth the while for such to see how Christianity justifies itself as the religion of fulfilled prophecy; and this all the more, since the self-testimony of Christianity, in the present condition of the investigation of the Scriptures, and in view of the restless sifting and decomposition of almost everything which has hitherto been accepted, must be more thoroughly revised, more exact, more many-sided, in many respects different, from that which was usual in earlier centuries, and which has been handed down even to the later missionary literature.

It is a delightful theme, a joyful work, in which we propose to be absorbed.[1] The Lord is in the process of coming in the Old Testament, in drawing near, in proclaiming His appearance, and we design to transport ourselves into this Old Testament period, and follow the steps of the One who is coming, pursue the traces of the One who is drawing near, seek out the shadows which He casts upon the way of His Old Testament

[1] This view, indeed, was not held by Schleiermacher, who, in his second *Sendschreiben* to Lücke, *Theologische Studien u. Kritiken*, Hamburg 1829, vol. ii. p. 497, says: "I can never consider this effort to prove Christ out of the Old Testament prophecies a joyful work, and am sorry that so many worthy men torment themselves with it."

history, and especially seek to understand the intimations of prophecy respecting Him.

The old theology made scarcely any distinction between the time of His coming and His entrance into the actual domain of history. The historical mode of view is a *charism*, granted to the Church in the period after the Reformation. We have reason to rejoice on this account. The Old Testament may be compared to the starry night, and the New Testament to the sunny day, or, as we may also say, the New Testament period, in its beginning, is related to the Old Testament as the coming of spring to winter. The spring in the kingdom of God suffered itself to be long waited for; and when at length spring days seemed to announce the end of the darkness and coldness of winter, the winter soon made its presence felt again. Then, however, when the Lord appeared, it became spring. He was indeed predicted as the embodiment of spring. Would, then, that in the following interpretations of Old Testament prophetic images there might also be fewer traces of the winter of life in which I stand, than of the spring-like freshness, of the living power, of the pentecostal nature of the subject of which I treat!

We live in an age, in which the Christian view of the world, through which the antique heathen view was overcome, threatens on its side to be overcome by the modern view of the world, which recognises no system of the world except that which is in accordance with natural laws, and no free miraculous interference of God in it. Christian truth, as it is attested in the Holy Scriptures, will also outlast this crisis. But since it must maintain its position against ever new antagonistic principles of advancing civilisation, culture, and science, it will be itself drawn into the process of development; for it stands indeed as firm as a rock which is not shaken by any dashing of the waves, yet not motionless as a rock, but it is living, and therefore, as regards the kind of life, is ever supplementing itself anew. It cannot be otherwise; since in Christ, as the apostle says, lie hidden all the treasures of wisdom and knowledge, hence the history of Christianity must be the history of the constant raising of these treasures. Christianity remains the same in its essence, but it is all the while more occupied with the depth of its essence, and ever coins new forms of thought and expression. Even in the age of Darwinism, and of his great discoveries in natural science, it will retain its unfading and inexhaustible power of life.

There is a crisis in the domain of the Bible, and especially in that of the Old Testament, in which the evening of my life falls. This crisis repels me on account of the joy of its advocates in destruction, on account of their boundless negations and their unspiritual profanity; but also this crisis, as so many crises since the time of the apostles, will become a lever for progressive knowledge, and it is therefore incumbent [upon us] to recognise the elements of truth which are in the chaos, and to gather them out; for as the primitive creation began with chaos, so in the realm of knowledge, and especially of spiritual life from epoch to epoch, that which is new goes forth from the chaos of the old. It is indeed not the business of an individual to complete this work of sifting and of refining and of reorganization. Nevertheless, we take part in it, although with a small degree of strength.

It is a depressing observation that Judaism has strong support in modern Christian theology, and that its literature is like an arsenal, out of which Judaism can secure weapons for its attack on Christianity. Nevertheless, in the midst of the present confusion we can be comforted with the consideration that this resource does not suffice for the maintenance of Judaism. For whether one takes with reference to Christianity the unitarian or trinitarian, the rationalistic or supernaturalistic standpoint, it is established that Christianity, as contra-distinguished from Judaism, is the religion of consummated morality, and that Jesus is the great holy divine man whose appearance halves the world's history. Christianity and the person of its founder are more to us than this, but we rejoice nevertheless in this firm position, which can bid defiance to all the attacks of Judaism, and in whose defence all who bear the name of Christ stand together. For every Christian as such, however he may understand the relation of the divine and the human in the person of Jesus, recognises in Jesus the end of Old Testament development, and in Christianity the completion of the religion of Israel.

We must admit that the treatment of our subject will vary, according as the one who treats it answers the question which Jesus once raised: "What think ye of Christ; whose son is He?" For the understanding of the process of becoming is dependent upon the conception of the goal; the understanding of the Old Testament process of becoming is dependent upon the truthful valuation of the person of Jesus. It is indeed just in this respect that we Christians are distinguished from the Jews: we do not expect any other; Judaism also does not really expect any other. Its hope of a Messiah, since the rejection of Jesus, the Christ of God, has sunk to a fantastic image of worldly patriotism, which has no power to warm the heart. We consider Jesus, on the contrary, as the end of the law, the goal of prophecy, the summit of Old Testament history, and with respect to the mystery of His twofold existence and work as mediator, we hold to His utterances respecting Himself, and to the testimony of His apostles; for a Christianity torn loose from these authorities, and otherwise understood, is only a scientific abstraction, an arbitrary excerpt according to a self-made pattern, an artificial product according to the demands of the spirit of the age. We are, so far as we are concerned, persuaded that gospels and epistles harmonize most intimately. We are certain of this, that in all essential points they admit of a reciprocal control. In the preparation for the New Testament in the Old, however, we are concerned with such essential points, the recognition of which is dawning, and which sometimes also breaks through like lightning. The noble ones in Beroea subjected even the word of the apostle to the test according to the Holy Scriptures which they had in their hands. We too shall see whether prophecy and the apostolic word reciprocally correspond and promote each other, so, indeed, that the Old Testament word of prophecy in relation to the New Testament dawn is only as the apostle says (2 Pet. i. 19): like "a lamp shining in a dark place."

INTRODUCTION.

---o---

§ 1. *The Twofold Character of the Problem expressed by the Name.*

IN all intellectual productions much depends upon finding the right name; for the name designates the goal, and indicates at the same time the way by which it is proposed to reach it. A suitable designation in itself would be: History of the Preparation for the Appearance of Jesus Christ in the Old Testament Consciousness; but the exegetical side of our problem does not in this way find the desired expression. Nor do we say "Old Testament Christology," because this designation leads us to expect a systematic rather than a historical and exegetical treatment. We therefore choose the title: "Messianic Prophecies in Historical Succession," because it affords expression both to the exegetical and historical side of the problem. It is true that our doctrinal material does not consist merely in predictions in the strict sense of the term, but the promises and hopes which have reference to the future salvation may be included under the conception of prophecy, for the promises of God are indeed pledged predictions, and the hope is established upon such sure prospects. The designation "Messianic" also appears to be too narrow, for in the domain of our theme are all such predictions which speak of the future salvation, without mentioning a human mediator by the side of the God of salvation. But in a wider sense we may nevertheless, as we shall see, call all those predictions Messianic which refer to the completion of the divine work of salvation, and of the divine kingdom in the Messianic age.

§ 2. *The Historical Significance of that which is apparently isolated.*

But can we from the passages of Scripture which lie before us form a history of the Messianic expectation of Israel with respect to a future salvation? These passages of Scripture are, indeed, like isolated points without connecting lines, and they are testimonies, not of the people, but of individuals among the people, so that we are not able to determine their effect upon the belief and hope of the mass. This doubt must be considered, but disappears on a further investigation of the subject. All progress in civilisation in the human race is accomplished through individuals, whose new discoveries and attainments become new impulses for the advancing dominion of man over the world of nature, and for their advancing spiritual culture. This is also true of religious progress; in every place where this takes a new turn, it has been men who were far beyond their age within whom this new turn has been accomplished. All religions which deserve this name, as express representations of Deity, and the right mode of worshipping Him, are to be traced back to single individuals who have founded them or transformed tham. That which has finally become common property was first a possession of individuals; but it will never be common property to the extent, that it will penetrate all the members of the people, or of the religious society in complete purity and original power. We need not be surprised if the Christological development, which goes through the Old Testament, is like a path of light, which consists of rays of light proceeding from single points of light. Moses, David, Isaiah—these are, above all others, the three whose profound natures, filled by the Spirit, were the source of the light of the Old Testament religion. We know, indeed, and if we did not know it, we must presuppose it, that the vital cognitions which went out from them were adopted only by the kernel of the people in consciousness and life. The condition of the mass was like a dark cloud which was irradiated by the light of revelation, but was not absorbed by it. But this is not prejudicial to the historical character and the execution of our task. We shall describe the gradual rising of the light as we represent the Christological development, whose essence is not conditional through a successful result; for as the true light appeared the darkness did not comprehend it.

§ 3. *The Indispensableness of Literary and Historical Criticism.*

Those great personalities of the history of revelation have no other way of being known to us than in the Old Testament Scriptures. The knowledge of them is mediated, partly through writings which relate concerning them, partly through writings which go back to them. In the former case we must raise the question, to what period the accounts belong, and whether they are credible; in the latter case, whether the works in question are authentic, that is, really have those persons as authors to whom they are ascribed. The course of development of the Christological views cannot therefore be mediated without the co-working of literary criticism and historical criticism, and all critical questions even here give way in significance in comparison with the Pentateuchal question, which in all directions is the fundamental and chief question of the Old Testament. We shall not avoid the influence of modern criticism in unwarranted self-confidence or in childish fear—we shall also use criticism, but without employing the grounds of decision which are now common, and which from principle deny objective reality to everything that is supernatural, and especially to the spiritual miracle of prophecy.

§ 4. *The Reasonableness of the Supernatural.*

While we recognise the supernatural factor in the

Old Testament history of redemption and in the history of the recognition of redemption, we proceed from the presupposition that the supernatural would be subject to the suspicion of that which is mythical and purely subjective if it merely belonged to the past and had no present. There is not only a kingdom of nature in which the natural laws of the system of the world have sway, but also a kingdom of freedom, that is, the reciprocal working of God and of the free creatures, in which a moral system of the world, which interferes in the course of nature and makes it serviceable to itself, has sway. The ultimate goal of this divinely-ordained reciprocal relation can be inferred. If a difference exists between the absolute God and all other beings as His creatures, the history of finite personal beings can have no other true and final goal than an ever deeper entrance into a living communion with God. A continuance in this way is, however, not possible without an actual interchange between God and these His creatures. Man must direct words and deeds to God which He understands; and, on the other hand, God must make Himself known to men in disclosures and acts which he distinguishes in the midst of the course of the laws of nature as the free inworking of the absolute God. The divine necessity of this reciprocal relation follows with necessity from the universal impulse of mankind to prayer; and the reality of this reciprocal relation is proved to every man who stands in living relation to God, through his experiences in prayer, and through the admonishing, warning, comforting voices of God, which he perceives in himself.

§ 5. *The Redemption a Logical Necessity.*

But man is caught in the toils of sin; not only individuals of the race, but also the race as a species, has incurred the penalty of sin and death, and has been driven from their moral duty of a continual approach to God into alienation from Him. If, nevertheless, mankind is to attain the end of their creation, it cannot take place without their being released from the labyrinth of their lost condition through sin, and without their being brought again into the path which leads to the goal of their creation. The work of salvation concerns mankind, and is designed for every individual, so that all who wish to be saved can be. The conclusion is not mathematically certain that this is to be the course of human history, for God is absolutely free, and He is under no law except His own will. But nevertheless it is logically necessary for us, that the final end for which God has created man can in no way be frustrated. He is indeed the omniscient One. As such He has foreseen that man would fall through sin from his vocation. We must therefore suppose, that if He had not determined to raise man again from his fall, He would not have created him at all. These are thoughts whose logical necessity is apparent, but which would not come into our minds if we did not know from the

Holy Scriptures, as the record of the will and way of God, that God the Creator is also God the Redeemer, who, on account of His decree before the foundation of the world, nevertheless brings human history, in spite of sin, to its culmination.

§ 6. *Messianic Prophecy with and without mention of the Messiah.*

The religion of revelation is the religion of redemption, planned by God the Creator from eternity. The Old Testament religion is the religion of the redemption believed and hoped for as future, and the New Testament religion is the religion of the redemption which was fundamentally consummated by the Mediator who appeared in the fulness of time. Faith is, in both Testaments, faith in God the Creator and Redeemer. The recognition of human mediation, through which God accomplishes the redemption, came only gradually about by means of an intricate process of development. But that the redemption is to be mediated in a human way is even in itself to be presupposed. God's help in behalf of the multitude of men is ever to make individuals, or one an instrument for many, as appears in the fact that God elected a people from the midst of the peoples, as a mediator, in attestation of Himself, and of the redemption of mankind from the labyrinth of idolatry. It must be admitted that this nationalizing of the religion obstructed and endangered the recognition of the universal and spiritual character of the work of redemption. The opposition in which Judaism until the present day remains to Jesus the Christ, actually proves how great a danger this unavoidable nationalizing brought with it. But the history of the Messianic prophecies, which we shall describe, is designed to show, that in spite of appearances to the contrary, the Saviour who has gone forth out of Israel in the person of Jesus is the end of Old Testament leadings, and the fulfilment of the deepest pre-Christian hopes and longings.

§ 7. *Messianic Prophecies in the Narrowest Signification.*

The high priest is called an anointed one in the Pentateuchal Torah, because he, and only he, not the other priests, was set apart for his office by anointing —that is, through the pouring of oil upon the head (Lev. viii. 12, cf. v. 30). The expression הַכֹּהֵן הַמָּשִׁיחַ, Lev. iv. 3 [the anointed priest], signifies the same as הַכֹּהֵן הַגָּדוֹל [the great priest]. The post-Biblical language (perhaps also even in Dan. ix. 26, if Onias III. is there intended, after whose removal, 171 B.C., Antiochus Epiphanes plundered the temple) also calls him simply מָשִׁיחַ, as when, in *Horayoth* 8ª, there is a discrimination between מָשִׁיחַ, נָשִׂיא, יָחִיד, private man, prince, and high priest. But outside of the Torah it is the king of Israel who is called the anointed, and indeed the anointed of Yahweh, *e.g.* Saul, 1 Sam. xii. 3; David, Ps. xviii. 51, 2 Sam. xxiii. 1; Zedekiah,

Lam. iv. 20; also Cyrus is honoured in Isa. xlv. 1 with the title of an anointed one of Yahweh, because Yahweh has brought about his elevation as king, and has chosen him as His instrument. For מָשַׁח signifies not only to anoint (*i.e.* to pour oil upon, or to apply oil in some other way), but has, aside from the external ceremonial completion of the anointing, the further meaning of anointing through word and deed (1 Kings xix. 16; Ps. cv. 15). In the time of the Judges, in which there was no united government of the entire people, it was a divinely-anointed king to whom hope and promise were directed; and when in the time of the Kings the kingdom went counter to its divinely-determined end (as, for example, in the time of Ahaz), promise and hope were directed all the more earnestly to a divinely-given righteous and victorious king. Messianic prophecies in the narrowest signification are accordingly such prophecies, as connect the hope of salvation and the glory of the people of God with a future king, who, proceeding from Israel, subjects the world to himself. This ideal king—that is, the one who completely actualizes the theocratic idea—is as such מָשִׁיחַ יְהוָה; but this is not yet the distinguishing characteristic name in the Old Testament. It is, for example, questionable whether in Hab. iii. 14, מְשִׁיחֶךָ refers to the present king or to the great One of the future; and in general there is no Old Testament passage in which מָשִׁיחַ indicates the future One with eschatological exclusiveness (not even Dan. ix. 25, where, as it appears, מָשִׁיחַ נָגִיד is intended of the

18 MESSIANIC PROPHECIES IN HISTORICAL SUCCESSION.

priestly king of the future).[1] This only can be certainly held, that even the congregation of the exilic period understood by the divinely-anointed One in Ps. cxxxii. and Ps. ii. the King of the final period.

§ 8. *The New Testament Glorification of the Conception of the Messiah.*

First, in the doctrinal language of post-Biblical Judaism the future One is called, almost with the significance of a proper name, מָשִׁיחַ, Greek *Μεσσίας*,[2] after the Aramaic form of the name מְשִׁיחַ, or with the post-positive article מְשִׁיחָא. Although the royal dignity is involved in מָשִׁיחַ when this word is used as a noun, the Targums and the literature of the Talmudical period prefer the designation מַלְכָּה מְשִׁיחָא, Heb. מֶלֶךְ הַפָּשִׁיחַ (when both are blended together like a proper name, as in מֶלֶךְ יְהוָה צְבָאוֹת, Zech. xiv. 16 f.); but sometimes simply מָשִׁיחַ, Aramaic מְשִׁיחַ, is found.[3] In the

[1] Luther translates Dan. ix. 25: "Until Christ the Prince," and also ver. 26: "And after sixty-two weeks Christ will be destroyed."—This is the only place in the Old Testament where he has used the name of Christ.

[2] De Lagarde holds that Μεσσίας is the Greek form of מָשִׁיחַ, a trans-Jordanian Arabic nominal form like שָׂעִיר for שָׂעִיר. It is, however, the Greek form of מְשִׁיחָא; the ח remaining unexpressed between the two long vowels as in $μιδα$ = מְחִידָא, Neh. vii. 54, and Μεσίας or Μεσσίας was written like 'Αβεσαλώμ or 'Αβεσσαλώμ, since through duplication greater stability was given to the short vowel.

[3] See *e.g. Lev. rabba* c. xiv.: "The Spirit of God brooded over the waters זה רוח של מלך המשיח." And without the article *Pesachim* 54ª, according to which שמו של משיח belong to the

INTRODUCTION. 19

so-called Psalms of Solomon, which were written in Hebrew about the year 48,—the year of the battle of Pharsalias,—and which have been preserved for us in a Greek translation which is to some extent difficult to understand, the future One is called (xvii. 36, xviii. 8) Χριστὸς κύριος (as in Luke ii. 11; Hebrew מָשִׁיחַ הָאָדוֹן). Even in the Septuagint Χριστός is the translation of the Hebrew מָשִׁיחַ. While, however, the New Testament designation of Jesus is coextensive with the Hebrew and Jewish מָשִׁיחַ philologically, it is not really; for, since the name Χριστός becomes the name of Jesus, it gives to the personality of Jesus its Old Testament stamp, not, however, without at the same time receiving a new stamp from Him. The name Χριστός receives a wider, deeper, more exalted meaning. It experiences in the light of the Saviour a metamorphosis (glorification). The royal idea which it expresses is not removed, but it is relieved of its one-sidedness. It indicates the Son of God and the Son of man, who, as the reward of His priestly self-sacrifice, receives the royal crown instead of the crown of thorns, and as the risen and exalted One rules the world, hence in a manner worthy of God, at whose right hand He sits.

Remark 1.—Within the course of the evangelical history the Lord is called Ἰησοῦς. First after God

seven things which preceded the Creation. And *Sanhedrin* 93[b], says Simeon, called Bar-Cochba: אֲנָא מָשִׁיחַ. *Targ. jer.* to Gen. xlix. 11 may serve as a proof passage for מלכא משיחא, which occurs frequently in the Targums: "How beautiful is מלכא משיחא, who shall one day rise from the house of Judah!"

raised Him from the dead, and, as is said in Acts ii. 36, made Him both Lord and Christ, He receives in addition to the proper name 'Ἰησοῦς the designation of honour, which has likewise become a proper name, Χριστός. Within the Gospels, however, except in John i. 17, xvii. 3, this double designation occurs only in Matt. i. 1, 18 (but here with the article prefixed τοῦ 'Ἰησοῦ Χριστοῦ); Mark i. 1. Aside from John xvii. 3 the evangelists write this double designation over the gates of their Gospels like a summary or emblem of the entire following history, with a similar signification as when the Torah prefixes the double designation יְהוָה אֱלֹהִים to Gen. ii.–iii. Both names express everything. In the name Jesus the idea of salvation predominates; in the name Christ, that of glory. We can say: the course in the Old Testament leads from Christ to Jesus, the course in the New Testament from Jesus to Christ.

Remark 2.—In spite of the one-sidedness of the royal image the royal dominion still remains one side in the image of the future One; and far from denying the royal dignity of His Messiahship, Jesus answers the question of Pilate (Mark xv. 2): σὺ λέγεις, and over His cross stands: ὁ βασιλεὺς τῶν 'Ἰουδαίων (Mark xv. 26), which the Jews would have liked to have changed, because He was not the King of the Jews, but said that He was (John xix. 21 f. Observe that this is the Gospel of John). But the kingdom which lies at the end of His course, while it embraces the world, is nevertheless not a worldly kingdom. He will one day be King of the Jews, and will again raise up the kingdom of Israel, but not before the Jewish people have subjected themselves to His sceptre in penitence and faith. As Yahweh became the King of Israel at Sinai when they accepted the law with the words נַעֲשֶׂה וְנִשְׁמָע,—we will perform and be obedient,—so Jesus will become King of Israel when, worshipping Him, they render Him homage; but even then He will not be a king in an external, earthly, narrow, and national way, as unspiritual natural pride dreams; for the kingdom of God in Christ is a $\beta a\sigma\iota\lambda\epsilon ia\ \tau\hat{\omega}\nu\ o\dot{\upsilon}\rho a\nu\hat{\omega}\nu$, that is, of heavenly origin and heavenly nature.

§ 9. *Messianic Prophecies in a Broader Signification.*

Even in the Old Testament the royal image of the future Anointed One is proved to be one-sided and inadequate, since it is neither coextensive with the need of salvation, nor exhausts the expectation of salvation. But not this alone. Since the idea of the God-man is first announced in single rays of light, the Mediator of salvation, in general, does not yet stand in the centre of Old Testament faith, but the completion of the kingdom of God appears mostly as the work of the God of salvation Himself with the recession of human mediation. But we also classify these prophecies under the general conception of Messianic, because indeed in the history of fulfilment it is God in Christ who from Israel works out and secures for mankind the highest spiritual blessings. Our prayer to Christ is prayer to God revealed in the flesh. Therefore, from a historical point of view, we regard the prophecies concerning the ultimate salvation, which are even silent concerning the Messiah, as Christological.

§ 10. *Historical Sketch of the Subject.*

The New Testament references to Old Testament prophecies are limited, rather accidentally than designedly, by the occasions afforded in the Gospel history and the apostolic trains of thought. Hence it has come to pass, that many Messianic passages of prime importance have remained unnoticed, *e.g.* Isa. ix. 5, 6 ; Jer. xxiii. 5, 6 ; Zech. vi. 12, 13. A richer and, to a certain extent, more systematic discussion of the predictions and representations concerning Christ in the Old Testament begins with the Epistle of Barnabas (71–120 A.D.), which is related to the Epistle to the Hebrews, but which stands far below it, and in Justin's Dialogue with Trypho (d. about 163 A.D.). This is, to a certain extent, a missionary document, the only one of the ancient Church, which breathes a spirit of love that seeks the lost, of which we can discover but little in the First Book of Cyprian's *Testimonia adversus Judaeos*[1] (d. 258), and in the *Altercatio Simonis Judaei et Theophili Christiani.*[2] Justin is in so far inferior to his Jewish opponent, that he is acquainted with the Old Testament only through the secondary source of the Septuagint. On the other hand, Origen (d. 254), who, in his Eighth Book, written against Celsus

---

[1] See W. Faber in *Saat auf Hoffnung*, Erlangen 1887, vol. xxiv. pp. 26–29.

[2] See Gebhardt-Harnack's *Texten und Untersuchungen*, Leipzig, i. 3.

(about 247), contends against the heathen and Jewish misrepresentations of the person of Christ and of Christianity, is acquainted with Hebrew, but his interpretation of the Scriptures suffers from his effort at that arbitrary allegorization in which the Alexandrian school is the successor of Philo. Nevertheless, the historical method of the Antiochian school brought about a reaction, which even referred direct Messianic prophecies like Micah v. 1 to Zerubbabel and in general to objects before Christ, and only, with reference to the result of their higher fulfilment, to Christ. Theodore of Antioch (d. 428), bishop of Mopsuestia, did this in a rash and offensive way. It was not taken into account by the ancient Church, down to the time of the Middle Ages, that there is in the Old Testament a preparation for the salvation in Christ through a connected and progressive history.[1] Nor was it taken into account in the time of the Reformation, when the predominantly anti-Judaistic, apologetic interest of the ancient Church was replaced by one which was predominantly dogmatic, and a spiritualistic interpretation took the place of an allegorical, which removed the national elements of the old prophecy by means of a symbolical or a mystical interpretation. First, Spener (d. 1705) and his school made way for a better understanding of the prophecies, while, with reference to Rom. xi. 25, 26, he recognised that which is relatively authorized in the national form of the Old

[1] In this connection special attention is called to Abelard's (d. 1142) *Dialogus inter Philosophum, Judaeum et Christianum.*

Testament prophecy. John Albert Bengel (d. 1752) and Christian Augustus Crusius (d. 1775) began to modify the stiff idea of inspiration, since they regarded the prophets not only as passive, but also at the same time as active instruments, and placed their range of view under the law of perspective. With Cocceius (d. 1669) began the method of treating the Old Testament in periods. But they were not able to divide this history into periods according to its internal development, in which chance and plan, freedom and necessity interpenetrate. When then rationalism, for which the way had been prepared by the Arminian Grotius (d. 1645), and Spinoza in his *Tractatus theologico politicus* (1670), and which was founded by Semler (d. 1791), degraded Jesus to a teacher of religion and morals, the Messianic prophecies of the Old Testament became almost entirely without an object, until the gradual unfolding of the idea of the Messiah was recognised in them, and, as there was a return from a merely nominal Christianity to that established by documents, the gradual subjective preparation of the essential salvation was acknowledged. This revolution was established by Hengstenberg's (d. 1869) *Christologie des Alten Testaments* (in three volumes, Berlin 1829-1835, second edition 1854-1857), which formed a new epoch in the treatment of the subject, followed in a spirit of freer criticism by Tholuck's (d. 1877) work, *Die Propheten und ihre Weissagungen*, Gotha 1860, and by Gustav Baur in his *Geschichte der alttestamentlichen Weissagung*, Theil 1, 1861. The proper mean between conservatism and progress was taken by Oehler (d. 1872) in his articles "Messias" and "Weissagung" in the first edition of Herzog's *Real-Encyklopädie*, vols. ix., Stuttgart 1858, and xvii., Gotha 1863, and in his *Theology of the Old Testament*,[1] which appeared after his death. The same praise is due to Orelli's work, *The Old Testament Prophecy of the Completion of the Kingdom of God*,[2] and to Briggs' *Messianic Prophecy*.[3] We should be guilty of inexcusable ingratitude if we were to make no mention of Hofmann's (d. 1877) work, which still remains unique, entitled *Weissagung und Erfüllung*, in two parts, Nördlingen 1841–1844. This treatise is a companion piece to Hengstenberg's *Christology*. The Old Testament account is here reconstructed historically and exegetically in a masterly way as an organic whole, developed in word and deed until the time of Christ, with which the history of the fulfilment, as the other half, reaching to the end of the present dispensation, is joined together. Many views of truth which have come into the modern scriptural theology have sprung from this original work, whose main fault is the straining of the type at expense of the prophecy. In his conception of the prophecies concerning Israel's future Hofmann's standpoint is realistic. He leaves the conception of Israel in the national estimation of it, without understanding by it the Church gathered out of Israel and the heathen, nevertheless in such

[1] First edition, Tübingen, 1873-74 ; second edition, 1882-85.
[2] Edinburgh.   [3] Edinburgh 1886.

a way as to exclude the restoration of all which cannot be harmonized with the Christian denationalizing of the religion and the doing away with the law. Also Bertheau in his lengthy article, "Die alttestamentliche Weissagung von Israel's Reichsherrlichkeit in seinem Lande," in the fourth volume of the *Jahrbücher für deutsche Theologie*, Gotha 1859, seeks to separate the present idea of the fulfilment from the particular national form. In like manner Riehm (d. 1888) in his work, *Die Messianische Weissagung*, Gotha 1875, which fails to do justice to the words of prophecy with reference to the conversion of Israel. The rationalistic standpoint, in which the historical method is carried out, is represented by Stähelin's work, *Die Messianischen Weissagungen*, Berlin 1847; Anger's lectures, published after his death (d. 1866), edited by Krenkel, *Ueber die Geschichte der Messianischen Idee*, Berlin 1873; Hitzig (d. 1875) in his *Vorlesungen über biblische Theologie und Messianischen Weissagung des Alten Testaments*, Karlsruhe, 1880, issued by Kneucher; and Kuenen's work, *The Prophets and Prophecy in Israel*, London 1877, which is distinguished more for its learning and sharp apprehension of the subject than for originality and genius, which, on principle, dismisses all that is supernatural as unhistorical, and regards ethical monotheism as the kernel of prophecy. Duhm's *Die Theologie der Propheten*, Bonn 1875, is peculiar in this respect, that he sets out with the proposition that the Old Testament literary prophets belong to an earlier age than the Mosaic law, and that in the writing of every prophet there is a special system of teaching, by means of which he hinders or helps the progress to greater freedom in religious things. In opposition to this rationalistic standpoint Edward König in his work, *Den Offenbarungsbegriff des Alten Testaments*, Leipzig 1882, defends the supernatural character of Old Testament prophecy.

A sketch of the history of the interpretation of Old Testament prophecy is given by Tholuck in his *Das Alte Testament im Neuen*, in the Supplement to his commentary on the Epistle to the Hebrews, and especially in the sixth edition, 1868; also in Oehler's article, entitled "Weissagung," in the first edition of Herzog's *Real-Encyklopädie;* and its progress since Bengel is given in Delitzsch's work, *Die biblisch-prophetische Theologie, ihre Fortbildung durch Chr. A. Crusius und ihre neueste Entwickelung seit der Christologie Hengstenberg's*, Berlin 1845. Many materials bearing upon the subject are afforded in Diestel's (d. 1879) *Geschichte des Alten Testaments in der christlichen Kirche*, Jena 1869.

Remark.—The representation of the course of development in prophecy will differ according as the supernatural factor of the history is recognised or not recognised by the writer as specifically different, and yet at the same time as historical, and Christianity as only the religion of perfect morality, or as the religion of redemption. But also aside from this, the representation will differ according to the position of the writer with reference to the results of modern literary historical criticism, and the new construction of the Old Testament history which is based upon it.

It is a postulate of our consciousness, that human history is engaged in a movement toward a definite end. This movement, far from being absolutely in a straight line, takes place under all kinds of deviations and retrogressons, and the valuation of that which is new is wont to be different, not only on the part of contemporaries, but also on the part of those who come later, since it does not treat of the things of nature, but rather of those of the spiritual life. Nevertheless there arises, in spite of all these devious ways, and notwithstanding the uncertainty of judgment, the demand for actual progress. And in view of the revolution which has taken place in the domain of Biblical investigation, the question is justified, what permanent religious advantage is to proceed from it.

All recognition of the truth is of a religious character, so far as God Himself is the truth, and the endless background of the recognition of all religious truth. Biblical questions, however, are immediately religious. I shall not presume to determine in advance that which in the year 2000 will be considered pure gold, which will have endured the smelting fire of criticism, and will have been won by means of it; but one thing we know, that the Holy Scriptures of the Old and New Testaments will be and will remain the document of the revelation of the one true God. And since the Old Testament religion is a preparation and a preliminary step for the New, we shall not take any offence if in the Old Testament Scriptures, which have the character of an effort to attain perfection, much appears more imperfect than before.

MESSIANIC PROPHECIES IN HISTORICAL SUCCESSION.

CHAPTER I.

THE DIVINE WORD CONCERNING THE FUTURE SALVATION BEFORE THE TIME OF THE PROPHETS.

§ 1. *Justification of the Beginning in Genesis* iii.

IF the historical succession, in which we propose to treat the Messianic prophecies, were to be understood as a succession in literary history, we should only be justified in beginning with Gen. iii., if we considered the so-called Jehovistic book, from which the history of Paradise is drawn, the oldest Old Testament historical book. But this is not our opinion. We consider it a very old historical source, older than modern criticism concedes, but not the oldest. Nevertheless we are justified in beginning with Gen. iii. For the narrative concerning the primitive condition and fall of man was not invented by the narrator, but was an old "*sage*" found by him, which he communicates to us in a form in which, stripped of its heathen mythological accessories, it has sustained the criticism of the Spirit of revelation. We may therefore begin where the documentary sacred history begins, since it contributes not a little to its recommendation, that although recorded by an Israelitish pen, it begins, not with a nation, but with mankind. The Biblical primitive history is the history of mankind, and does not have the peculiar national and mythological colours of the primitive traditions outside of Israel. But does not the narrative in Gen. ii., iii. sound mythical? If we understand by myth (*mythus*) the investiture, not only of universal thoughts, but also of definite realities in symbolical dress, we may nevertheless regard the history of Paradise as a myth, so far only as we hold fast the following as realities:—(1) that there was a demoniacal evil one, before evil had taken possession of man; (2) that this demoniacal evil one was the power of temptation before which man fell; (3) that God after mankind had fallen punished them, but at the same time opened a way of salvation, by which they could again secure communion with God; (4) that He placed before them in prospect the victory over that power of temptation through which they had lost the communion with God in Paradise.

Remark. — Also in the Babylonian "sage" the serpent is *Tiâmat* (*Tihâmat*), the source of all evil, the personified תְּהוֹם. This expresses a profound thought, since the essence of evil is the falling back into the natural elements, out of which the world in mankind is raised to the image of God. The serpent is called *aibu* (the enemy, אֹיֵב), κατ' 'εξ.; it is called *ṣêru* = *maḫḫu* (*rabbu*), like ὁ δράκων ὁ μέγας in the New Testament Apocalypse. It seduces mankind to sin, since it seeks to sustain itself in its authority. It is also said of it, that it destroyed the grove of life.[1] Much here is uncertain. In comparison, the Iranian "sage" is far clearer, according to which the serpent is the first creation of Ahriman, who himself is both represented and called a serpent. The serpent disturbs the peace, destroys paradise, and casts down Yima, the ruler of the golden age, that is, the first man. We have here reminiscences, which are worthy of attention, respecting the origin of evil, although in a mythical garb.

§ 2. *Beginning and Object of the Theophanies.*

Between us and God there is now a wall of separation. God has become far from us, and is concealed, as it were, behind an impenetrable veil. The "sagen" of the [different] peoples testify in many ways, that at the beginning of human history God was immediately near to man, and had intercourse with him, and that our present distance from God is a loss. It follows from our present nature that we cannot make any representation to ourselves of that original intercourse of God with men. Even in Gen. ii., iii. we are not raised above this inability of representing it. The narrative retains a mysterious background, but it has a transparent deep meaning. After the fall, which destroyed the union of God and man, man perceives the steps of God, who is drawing near, and flees from Him. He comes indeed as a Judge who is to be feared,

[1] See Friedrich Delitzsch, *Paradies*, p. 87 ff.; and *Assyrische Lesestücke*, p. 95 ff.: *Texte zur Weltschöpfung und zur Auflehnung und Bekämpfung der Schlange Tiamat*.

not, however, to destroy for the sake of punishing, but through bitter chastisement to win back the lost. And in a significant manner the one who appears is called Yahweh-Elohim. God, as Creator of the entire creation and as its Finisher (*Vollender*), that is, as the Power which finally fills it completely with glory (1 Cor. xv. 28), is called אֱלֹהִים; and God as Redeemer, that is, as Mediator of this completion (*Vollendung*) through sin and wrath, is throughout called יַהְוֶה.[1] His audible steps after the fall are His first steps toward the goal of the revelation in the flesh (1 Tim. iii. 16), which is the restoration and completion of the immanence of divine love in the world.

§ 3. *The Primitive Promise.*

Thus presenting Himself, God announces their sentence to the serpent, to the woman, and to Adam— to these three together, as concerned in their solidarity.

The serpent, and in it the spiritual being, whose mask it became, or if we understand the account mythically, whose image it is, are cursed on account of the temptation which proceeded from them, which plunged mankind into sin and death. The earth is

---

[1] [This is a liberty which we are compelled to take. Most of the Hebrew words in the German text are unpointed. Prof. Delitzsch, however, never pronounced יהוה, Jehovah, which he considered a philological monstrosity. But, as in the transliteration which he has given of the name, he could only recommend his students to say Yahweh, or to follow the example of the Jews in reading Adhonai.]—C.

cursed on Adam's account, while the natural world, after its destiny as a means of blessing to mankind has been thwarted, is turned into an instrument of wrath against them. Adam himself, however, is not cursed, but in the midst of the curse on the tempter the hope of a victory in the contest with the power of evil rises upon mankind. The verdict pronounced upon the serpent, after it has been humbled to a worm in the dust, is (iii. 15): "And I will put enmity between thee and the woman, and between thy seed and her seed." The woman, as the one first seduced, and the serpent, who served the seducer as an instrument, are here representatives of their entire race. The divine retribution places, that is, establishes, between the race of serpents and of men a relation of internal and actual enmity. And who will conquer in this war, which is enacted as a law of the further history ? " He shall crush thee on the head, and thou shalt crush him on the heel." In no Semitic idiom does שׁוּף have the signification of שָׁאַף, to snap, or look eagerly for something; and never is שָׁאַף, or indeed any verb indicating a hostile disposition, construed with a double accusative. This construction with the accusative of the person, and the part which is affected, is peculiar to verbs which indicate a violent meeting, *e.g.* הִכָּה, *to smite;* רָצַח, *to murder.* Hence שׁוּף, which is repeated, neither has the first nor the second time the meaning of *lying in wait* (Septuagint, τηρεῖν; Jerome, *insidiari*). The verb שׁוּף is used by the Targum for דְּכָּא, *to crush;* טְחַן, *to grind to powder;* שָׁחֵק *to pulverize.*

It has the meaning which is there presupposed also in Job ix. 17 (on the contrary, neither the meaning *inhiare* nor *conterere* is suited to Ps. cxxxix. 11), and the signification of the root שוף (שפ), *terere, to grind*, is confirmed through an extensive tribe of Semitic words, according to which among the old [versions] the translation is given by the Samaritan and Syriac. Only when we translate it: "He (the Seed of the woman) shall crush thee on the head" ($\sigma u\nu\tau\rho\acute{\iota}\psi\epsilon\iota$, Rom. xvi. 20), does the sentence include the definite promise of victory over the serpent, which, because it suffers the deadly tread, seeks to defend itself, and sinking under the treader is mortally wounded (Gen. xlix. 17).

§ 4. *The Primitive Promise in the Light of Fulfilment.*

It is the entire decree of redemption which is epitomized in this original word of promise, so far as we only maintain that the serpent as a seducer is intended, and that the curse, which falls upon it, has a background with reference to the author of the seduction. The malignant bite of the serpent in the heel of men, which they retaliate in the midst of their defeat by treading on its head, is only a natural picture of that which ever constitutes the most central purport of history—namely, the conflict of mankind with Satan, and with all who are $\dot{\epsilon}\kappa \ \tau o\hat{u} \ \delta\iota a\beta\acute{o}\lambda o u \ (\pi o\nu\eta\rho o\hat{u})$; for, after the power of grace has entered mankind by means of the promise, they are placed, through the fall, in the attitude of a second decision for themselves, which will result in such a way, that many of the seed of the woman who had the promise, separate themselves, and take a position on the side of the serpent. The promise indeed has reference to mankind as a race, for the word הוּא refers to זֶרַע אִשָּׁה. Nevertheless, since the promise of victory refers to that serpent from whom the seduction went forth, hence to the victory over the one seducer (ὁ ὄφις ὁ ἀρχαῖος), we may consequently infer that the seed of the woman will culminate in One in whom the opposition will be strained to the utmost; and the suffering in the struggle with the seducer will rise to the highest pitch, and the victory will end for ever in complete conquest. This primitive promise is also intended to be coextensive with the fulfilment; for Christ, the son of Mary, is the seed of the woman, γενόμενος ἐκ γυναικός (Gal. iv. 4), in a wonderfully unique way. Hence the new humanity, which has its head in Him, and which, through Him, stands in the relation of children to God, is indeed born of a woman, but in so far as it overcomes Satan is not begotten by man. This authority is not a work of nature, but a spiritual gift (John i. 12 f.). The entire history and order of salvation are unfolded in this protevangelium. Like a sphinx, it crouches at the entrance of sacred history. Later in the period of Israelitish Prophecy and Chokma, the solution of this riddle of the sphinx begins to dawn; and it is only solved by Him through whom and in whom that has been revealed towards which this primitive prophecy was aimed.

Remark 1.—But how is it consistent with the divine order of salvation that the meaning of the protevangelium, and in general of the history of the fall, should be first recognised so late, and should be first fully and completely disclosed through the New Testament revelation? It can only be explained on the supposition that the faith which brought salvation in the Old Testament was a faith in God the Redeemer. The deeper the Israelite felt the curse and the burden of sin, and was attacked on every side by sufferings and miseries, and was anxious on account of the darkness of death and of the next world, the more ardently he longed for redemption from sin and death, and especially from this evil world; and the faith in which he found rest was faith in God the Redeemer according to His promise. He longed for the visible revelation of the supramundane God—His coming down from heaven to earth; but that He would complete the work of redemption, through a man in whom He dwelt as the angel of the Mosaic redemption; that was an apprehension which was developed only gradually, and first became fully clear to faith in the face of Jesus Christ.[1]

Remark 2.—The Alexandrian Book of Wisdom ii. 24 says that through the envy of the devil death came into the world. Also in the Palestinian Jewish literature such gleams of light are found—Christian perceptions before Christ—which Judaism first gave up in opposition to Christianity; for (1) as the designation

[1] One of the most precious utterances of Bengel's is the following thesis: "Gradatim Deus in patefaciendis regni sui mysteriis progreditur sive res ipsae spectentur sive tempora. Opertum tenetur initio quod deinde apertum cernitur. Quod quavis ætate datur, id sancte debuit amplecti, non plus sumere, non minus accipere."

of the first man with אדם הקדמון (ὁ πρῶτος ἄνθρωπος Ἀδάμ, 1 Cor. xv. 45) is old Jewish, so also is the designation of the serpent which led man astray with נחש הקדמון (Ὁ ὄφις ὁ ἀρχαῖος, Rev. xii. 9, xx. 2); (2) the Palestinian Targum testifies that in Gen. iii. 15 there is promised a healing of the bite in the heel from the serpent, which is to take place "at the end of the days, in the days of King Messiah." In the Palestinian Midrash to Genesis [1] we read: "The things which God created perfect since man sinned have become corrupt (נתקלקלו), and do not return to their proper condition until the son of Perez (*i.e.* according to Gen. xxxviii. 29, Ruth iv. 18 ff., the Messiah out of the tribe of Judah) comes." According to this the Messiah is Saviour and Restorer, as the apostolic word says of Jesus (1 John iii. 8), that He has appeared, ἵνα λύσῃ τὰ ἔργα τοῦ διαβόλου.

§ 5. *First Effects and Verifications of the Primitive Promise.*

A first echo of the divine word, received in faith concerning the victory of mankind, is the name חַוָּה (Septuagint, ζωή), which Adam gives his wife; for— as the narrator explains (iii. 20*b*) the meaning and propriety of this name—she became "the mother of all living;" that is, in spite of death, the mother of each individual of the race, which is destined to live, to whom the victory over the power of the evil one is promised, and hence as mother of the Seed of the woman who is to crush the head of the serpent.

[1] *Bereshith rabba* xii.

We consider as a second echo the language of Eve when she became mother for the first time. Although this cannot possibly be understood as an expression of the belief that her first-born was the incarnate Yahweh, —for the terms of the primitive promise do not give any occasion for such an expression,—but must rather indicate that, with Yahweh as helper and giver, she has brought forth a man-child, which she has received as her own, nevertheless her exclamation stands related to iii. 15, since she designated God with the name of Yahweh, and in any case as the God of the promised salvation, for this Hebrew name of God belongs to the later period of the origin of the peoples. Through the marvel of this first birth she is placed in a joyful amazement, which is powerfully increased, because that thus the promise of the victory of the Seed of the woman appeared to be realized. But her first-born was the murderer of his brother; Cain was ἐκ τοῦ πονηροῦ (1 John iii. 12), he took his position on the side of the seed of the serpent. The religious congregation which was formed at the time of Enosh, the son of Seth, could already name one of their members as a martyr. When it is said, iv. 26, that at that time men began to call on and to call out the name of Yahweh,—that is, to pray together to God as Yahweh, and publicly to recognise Him as such,—this, too, stands in connection with iii. 15, for this historical notice is designed to indicate that men at that time joined a congregation which worshipped the God of the promised salvation. But if mankind is ever to be free from the bondage of sin, as is promised in iii. 15, they must likewise be free from the curse of death. The end of Enoch's life, the seventh from Adam in the line of Seth, shows that man, if he had proved true in the probation of free will, could have gone over into another stadium of existence without death and corruption. Death is, indeed, since the fall a law of nature; but God, who has enacted this law of nature, can also make it inoperative when He will through the exertion of His almighty power. The translation of Enoch, as well as of Elijah, is a prophecy in act of the future end of death (Isa. xxv. 8; 1 Cor. xv. 54). The primitive promise includes this end of death in itself, for the crushing of the serpent is the disarming of him "who has the power of death" (Heb. ii. 14).

Remark 1.—The impression that אֶת in אֶת־יָהְוֶה, iv. 1*b*, indicates the definite object, as vi. 10, xxvi. 34, is so strong that the Jerusalem Targum translates: "I have gotten a man, the Angel of Yahweh." But this interpretation cannot be maintained, for the reason that the Angel of Yahweh first enters into history and consciousness after the time of the patriarchs.

Remark 2.—Enoch announced, according to Jude, ver. 14, the parousia of the Lord in judgment. It is indeed in itself probable that Enoch, since he walked with God,—a commendation which only Noah shares with him, vi. 9,—also knew about the ways of God; but his prophecy, which Jude quotes, belongs to the "sage" (Haggada), and serves the author of the Epistle a didactic purpose. That it refers to the coming of the Lord in judgment, although the history of mankind had not begun so very long ago, is strange in itself. Not long after the beginning of the Church, the parousia of Christ as judge was longed and hoped for. The corruption through sin was so great at all times, that the believers longed that God, through a judicial interference, might help the Seed of the woman to a victory over the seed of the serpent.

§ 6. *The Expected Comforter.*

While in Lamech, the seventh from Adam within the Cainitic line, the worldly tendency of this line rises to blasphemous arrogance, there appears in Enosh, Enoch, and Lamech, the third, seventh, and ninth of the Sethitic line, an indigenous tendency toward the God of the promised salvation. Lamech, the Sethite, when his first son was born, hoped that in him, the tenth from Adam, the period of the curse would come to a comforting conclusion. This is evident from his elevated words when he says (v. 29): "This one shall comfort us for our work and for the toil of our hands [according to the signification of the Hebrew word: comforting, to make one free from painful work], because of the ground [*i.e.* that which the ground renders necessary] which Yahweh hath cursed." In this hope he calls him Noah, *i.e.* breathing out, rest (connected with נחם, to comfort, by causing to breathe out). The comfort which he expects from God through him is not comfort in words, but the comfort of an act of salvation. This comfort was also fulfilled through him, although not fully and in entirety, but in a way preparatory to the completion. The rainbow after the flood was a comfort, the blessing of which extended from that time on until the end. It pledged mankind, after the wrathful visitation in judgment, of their continuance, and of the dawn of a better time, in which, instead of wrath, a blessing predominates, a time of favour, patience, and long-suffering of God (Acts xvii. 30, xiv. 17 ; Rom. iii. 26). Noah is the first mediator of the sacred history, a mediator of comfort. Comfort (*nechama*) is one of the pregnant words in which all that is hoped from the God of salvation is combined. Yahweh, as Redeemer of His people, is called their Comforter, Isa. xlix. 13, lii. 9. And the Servant of Yahweh, the Mediator of salvation, explains it as His calling to comfort all that mourn, Isa. lxi. 2. Noah is a forerunner of this great Comforter, in whom all who labour and are heavy laden find rest to their souls.

Remark.— Comforter, מְנַחֵם, is an old synagogical designation for the Messiah; compare Schoettgen, *De Messia*, Dresdae 1742, p. 18. Jesus Himself is called παράκλητος, Comforter, for His promise, " He shall send you ἄλλον παράκλητον " (John xiv. 16), presupposes that Christ Himself is παράκλητος (מְנַחֵם=פְּרַקְלִיט).

§ 7. *The Promise of the Blessing of the Nations in the Seed of the Patriarchs.*

In Gen. ix. 24–27 we read how Noah in spirit penetrated the moral and fundamental character, and consequently the future, of the three groups of peoples springing from Canaan, Shem, and Japheth; and how he awards to Canaan the curse of servitude, to Japheth far-reaching political power, and to Shem a central religious significance which also draws Japheth to him. The God of salvation is the God of Shem; Shem is therefore for himself and the nations a bearer of the revelation of this God. According to this it is a Shemite whom God, after Noah, entrusts with the second epoch-making mediatorship. Abraham is chosen out of the midst of the nations to become a mediator of the revelation of salvation, and the promise of the salvation of the entire race is connected with him and his seed as centre, and starting-point: "And all the kindreds of the earth shall bless themselves in thee and in thy seed." This promise is made three times to Abraham (xii. 3, xviii. 18, xxii. 18), and once each to Isaac and Jacob (xxvi. 4, xxviii. 14). It is given three times with וְנִבְרְכוּ (xii. 3, xviii. 18, xxviii. 14), and twice with וְהִתְבָּרְכוּ (xxii. 18, xxvi. 4). It is questionable whether it should be translated as a passive: "they shall be blessed," or as a reflexive: "they shall bless themselves." The *Niphal* נִבְרַךְ occurs only in this promise, but the *Hithpael*, wherever it occurs, *e.g.* Jer. iv. 2, has a reflexive signification. Nevertheless, the Septuagint (Acts iii. 25; Gal. iii. 8) translates all of the five passages with a passive ἐνευλογηθήσονται. Since a longing desire for salvation, according to God's plan of salvation, is always accompanied with actual attainment, the sense remains essentially the same, whether we translate passively or reflexively. The promise makes Abraham and his seed possessors of a divine blessing, which is to become the end of the desire of all nations, and at the same time also their possession.[1] Israel is the seed of Abraham (Isa. xli. 9), as the people who mediate salvation (Isa. xix. 24; Zech. viii. 13); but this mediation of salvation comes to its final completion in Christ, the one descendant of Abraham, in whom the seed of Abraham, according to his calling as mediator of a blessing, finds its consummation.

Remark.—The inference of Paul from the singular בְּזַרְעֶךָ (Gal. iii. 16) has indeed a rabbinical character;[1] but the thought is perfectly correct, that the singular וּבְזַרְעֶךָ includes that which a plural would precisely exclude, namely, that the seed of Abraham, which is the means of a blessing, is a unity which will finally be concentrated in One; for זֶרַע can be just as well used of one (Gen. iv. 25) as of many. The poet of Ps. lxxii. begins in ver. 16 with the same idea: The promise of the blessing upon the peoples will be

[1] The Targum translates: "They shall be blessed through thee, through thy children, on account of thy merit, and of theirs" (זְכוּת). The Jewish doctrine of the merit of works casts its shadow into the understanding of the Scripture.

[2] In like manner the Mishna, *Sanhedrin* iv. 5, where it is remarked on דְּמֵי, Gen. iv. 10, "he does not say דַּם אָחִיךָ, but דְּמֵי אָחִיךָ: that is, his blood and the blood of his posterity," זרעותיו (plural of זֶרַע); cf. Abraham Geiger's article, "זְרָעִיּוֹת, זַרְעֲיָתָא, σπέρματα," in the *Zeitschrift der morgenländ. Gesellschaft*, Leipzig 1858, pp. 307–309.

fulfilled in King Messiah, whose name continues and buds forever. In this One the mediatorship of the blessing of the people of Abraham attains its consummation, nevertheless without its then having an end, since the blessing which is effected by One, and which going out from Him has extended over the nations of the earth, has not been secured without the co-operation of Israel, through the apostle from Israel. But since the One appeared, the mediatorship of salvation through Israel is conditioned in this way: that, first, it must be blessed by Him whose blessing, first of all, pertains to those who are children of the prophets and of the covenant (Acts iii. 25 f.).

CHAPTER II.

THE PROPHETIC BENEDICTIONS OF THE DYING PATRIARCHS.

§ 8. *Jacob's artful Procurement of the Blessing of the First-Born.*

CICERO says:[1] *Appropinquante morte [animus] multo est divinior.* It is an experimental fact that precisely through the approach of the night of death the most intense effulgence flashes through the human spirit, which has sprung from the being of God; and it is in connection with this psychological natural phenomenon that the patriarchs just before their death become seers, and utter testamentary words of a prophetic character concerning their children. Their blessings are not merely wishes, whose effect is coextensive with the granting of the prayer of faith, but they are at the same time predictions, which proceed from the divinely-mediated view into the future, as it has been decreed. Of such a sort is the blessing of the first-born, which Isaac utters regarding his second son, since Divine Providence frustrated that which his natural will intended. It arose from the divine promise which had already gone

[1] *De Divinatione,* lib. i. § 63.

forth, which Isaac had grasped in faith (Heb. xi. 20), and had further unfolded in the spirit of prophecy. This blessing of the first-born consists of four parts (xxvii. 27–29). It promises the one whom it concerns: (1) The possession of the land of Canaan under the divine benediction (vers. 27*b*, 28):

> See, the smell of my son
> Is as the smell of a field which
> Yahweh hath blessed.
> And God will give thee of the dew of heaven,
> And of the fat fields of the earth,
> And plenty of corn and must.

(2) The subjection of the nations, and indeed without limitation, in such general terms, that the limitation to the nations of Canaan, perhaps including the neighbouring countries, is contrary to the words of the text (ver. 29*a*):

> Peoples shall serve thee,
> And nations bow down to thee.

(3) The primacy over his brothers, that is, the tribes of Israel, and over those blood relations who were outside the posterity of the line of promise (ver. 29*b*):

> Be Lord over thy brethren,
> And thy mother's sons shall bow down to thee.

(4) So high a position in redemptive history, that blessings and curses are conditioned by the attitude which men take to him who has received the blessing (ver. 29*c*):

> Cursed be every one that curseth thee,
> And blessed be every one that blesseth thee.

PROPHETIC BENEDICTIONS OF PATRIARCHS. 49

When Esau, weeping bitterly, also begs for a blessing, he has for him, too, some promises, but of such a sort that they bring a dimness into the pure light of the blessing of Jacob, which is deserved through his artifice; but Isaac cannot recall any of the promises made to Jacob, for he knows that God has spoken through him, and that, against his own will, he has become God's instrument. It is the blessing of Abraham that Isaac, as if passing by himself, lays upon Jacob, for he promises him the possession of Canaan (cf. xii. 7) and victorious power (cf. xxii. 17); also the addition: "I will bless those that bless thee, and him that curseth thee will I curse," was already spoken to Abraham (xii. 3). The blessing and the curse of men are to be determined by the relation which they take to the one who has been blessed by God,—a determination which must have a deep moral ground, since the God of revelation is the holy One, who, as such, neither gives the preference in a partizan way nor promotes worldly pride of rank. Whoever blesses the patriarchs evinces thereby—as, for example, the blessing of Abram through Melchisedek shows (xiv. 19)—his belief in God, whose confessors they are. The salvation, which is finally to find its complete historical representation in the person of Jesus the Christ, has now, according to the measure of its stage of preparation, the patriarchs, His ancestors, as possessors and bearers.

§ 9. *The Designation of Judah as Royal and Messianic Tribe.*

After the three patriarchs had been enlarged from Jacob to twelve heads of tribes, the question arises, from which of the twelve tribes the promised salvation shall go forth. Jacob's prophetic blessing (Gen. xlix.) answers this question. Reuben, through his incest with Bilhah, had forfeited the right of primogeniture. It could not be transmitted to Simeon and Levi, on account of their outrage on the inhabitants of Shechem. Hence Jacob, in view of his near death, transfers the double inheritance (the בְּכֹרָה, in the narrower meaning of an inheritance), which is connected with the right of primogeniture, to Joseph, his favourite son, but primacy and the world-position in the history of salvation, to Judah, his fourth son (1 Chron. v. 1 f.). Jacob promises him the leadership of the tribes of his people as an inalienable right, won through his lion-like courage, until, on his coming to Shiloh, his dominion of the tribes should be enlarged to a dominion over the world:

8 Judah thee, thee shall thy brethren praise !
Thy hand is on the necks of thine enemies,
The sons of thy father shall bow down to thee.

9 Judah is a young lion,
From the prey, my son, thou art gone up :
He lies down, he couches as a lion, and as a lioness,
Who dares to wake him up ?

10 The sceptre shall not depart from Judah,
Nor the leader's staff from between his feet,
Until he comes to Shiloh ;
And to him will be the obedience of the peoples.

JUDAH AS ROYAL AND MESSIANIC TRIBE. 51

We understand יָבֹא שִׁילֹה in the sense which it has elsewhere; בּוֹא שְׁלֹה signifies to come to Shiloh (Josh. xviii. 9; 1 Sam. iv. 12), as הֵבִיא שְׁלֹה signifies to bring to Shiloh (Judg. xxi. 12; 1 Sam. i. 24); also, after הָלַךְ and שָׁלָה, שְׁלֹה, is used to indicate the place whither. It is also certain that שִׁילֹה is not a proper name, since, in vers. 11, 12, Judah is the subject, who, after he has fought his way through, rejoices in prosperous, happy peace in a land richly blessed with wine and milk, so that Judah also in ver. 10 must be the subject, without the interposition of another. And that which Jacob promised Judah actually came to pass. For as Israel, at whose head was the tribe of Judah, pitched the tent of the testimony in Shiloh, between Shechem and Bethel, hence in the heart of Canaan, the land, as is said in Josh. xviii. 1, was subdued before them: the conquest had made progress in a direction which, with persistent, similar energy, bore in itself the pledge of completion. But, furthermore, Judah really became the royal tribe in Israel, which, in David and Solomon, had command, not over the tribes of Israel alone, but also over the neighbouring peoples. The weakening and the breaking through of the power and permanence of the kingdom of Judah are relatively unimportant elements for the prophet. But since the Chaldean catastrophe made an end of the Davidic kingdom,—which arose in Zerubbabel after the exile only in a shadowy way and for a short time,—the fulfilment of the blessing concerning Judah would certainly lack its crown if the divinely-anointed One, to whom the Lord (Ps. ii. 8) gives the heathen for His inheritance, and the ends of the earth for His possession, had not arisen out of Judah. But it is evident, says the Epistle to the Hebrews (vii. 14), that our Lord sprang from Judah; and the Apocalypse, since it calls Him the Lion from the tribe of Judah (v. 5), points back to this blessing of Jacob. Hence the prediction concerning Judah remains Messianic, even when we understand Shiloh as the name of a place. Since Jacob names the tribe of Judah as the royal tribe of Israel, the preliminary history of the Messiah has advanced so far, that now Judah is chosen as the place for the appearance of the future One.

Remark 1.—When שִׁילֹה is understood as indicating a place, only the rendering preferred by Hitzig need be considered in connection with the one given above: " so long as they come to Shiloh," that is, from the standpoint of the speaker forever, since (according to this interpretation) he does not know any other central place of worship. But this supposition is contrary to history (Ps. lxxviii. 60 ff.), the generalizing of the subject of יָבֹא disturbs [the connection], the explanation of עַד כִּי through " as long as " (equivalent to עַד אֲשֶׁר) is contrary to the dominant idiom, which knows עַד כִּי only in the signification of *donec* or *adeo ut* (Gen. xxvi. 13; 2 Sam. xxiii. 10; 2 Chron. xxvi. 15), and this expedient in order to arrive at [the meaning] " forever " is unnecessary, since [the expression] " until that " frequently indicates (*e.g.* Gen. xxviii. 15) a climax and a culmination, beyond which that which is said does not cease, but continues, or even, as in the preceding case, is heightened. It is surprising that none of the ancient translators and intrepreters thought of שִׁילֹה as the city of Shiloh. This interpretation of the word first became current after Herder, who adopted it from W. G. Teller (1766). But we have a similar example in Lamech's Song of the Sword (Gen. iv. 23 f.). The significance of the blasphemous praise of the iron weapon was first perceived by Herder and Hamann.

Remark 2. — The ancient translators, who presuppose the reading שלה (without י, as in the Samaritan Pentateuch), take this שלה in the sense of שֶׁלּוֹ, and understand it either of a fact: "until that come which belongs to him" (to Judah), τὰ ἀποκείμενα αὐτῷ (Septuagint, Theodotion), namely, the dominion over the world; or personally: "until he comes, to whom it (the sceptre or the rule) belongs, ᾧ ἀπόκειται (Aquila, Symmachus, Onkelos, second Jerusalem Targum, Syrian). Perhaps Ezekiel (Ezek. xxi. 32) presupposes this interpretation of שלה, since he names the future ideal king אֲשֶׁר לוֹ הַמִּשְׁפָּט; in the Septuagint הַמִּשְׁפָּט is omitted, as it is simply rendered ᾧ καθήκει. But the following reasons may be urged against the meaning which has been incorporated with the word, as the one originally intended:—1. The abbreviation שׁ for אֲשֶׁר is foreign to the prose style of ancient Hebrew; there are only two uncertain references in support of it: (1) the combination of particles בְּשַׁגַּם (Gen. vi. 3, provided this reading is to be preferred to the dominant one בְּשַׁגָּם); (2) the name of the Levite מִישָׁאֵל (Ex. vi. 22, provided it signifies, like its synonym מִיכָאֵל, "who is like God?"). 2. Although the writing בֹּה

occurs once for בו (Jer. xvii. 24), לה is never found for לו. Moreover, the Massoretic reading שִׁילֹה excludes the supposition that שׁ is equivalent to אֲשֶׁר. In the Talmud, *Sanhedrin* 98b, it is read thus: for the pupils of Rabbi Shila (שילא) remark in honour of their teacher, that שִׁילֹה which sounds similarly is the name of the Messiah. We do not know how they interpreted it.[1]

It is a proof of the power of fashion even in exegesis, that several of the most recent exegetes have again taken up שלה as equivalent to שֶׁלּוֹ, which was heretofore considered as worthy of mention only as a matter of history. Driver and Briggs interpret according to the Septuagint: "until his own [that which belongs to Judah] shall come;" von Orelli: "until he [Judah] come into his own [the land of his inheritance],—an explanation which has not hitherto been set forth by any one, according to which שִׁילֹה is equivalent to אֶל־אֲשֶׁר־לוֹ; Wellhausen expunges וְלוֹ, and translates: "until he come to whom the obedience of the people belongs." Stade[2] goes still further than Wellhausen, as he expunges the entire tenth verse as a post-exilic addition; Kautzsch and Socin translate וְלוֹ, but under the impression of this modern confusion treat שִׁילֹה as untranslatable. And so it goes: the best and truest has the fortune gradually to become old, and people hasten after that which is new, until this also becomes old and they return to the old. The old [interpretation], which will ever reappear, is in the

[1] See G. H. Dalman, *Der leidende und der sterbende Messias der Synagoge*, 1888, p. 37. The word שילו occurs in the Talmudic proverb as the name of a man : שילו חטא ויוחנא משתלמא, Shilo has sinned and Johana must suffer for it.

[2] *Geschichte Israels*, Leipzig, 1887, vol. i. p. 160.

present case the understanding of שִׁילֹה יָבֹא in Josh. xviii. 9, and in other places where it occurs, in a geographical signification.

The name of the place (שִׁילֹה, שִׁילוֹ), defectively written שִׁלֹה (שִׁלוֹ), is formed from שׁל, שָׁלָה, to hang down in a flabby way, to be unstrung, to rest, and hence, as the gentile שִׁילֹנִי shows, contracted from שִׁילוֹן; it indicates stretching out, relaxation, recreation, rest,—certainly a fitting name of a place, and one which recommends itself. The form has the character of a proper name, as the name of a man, שְׁלֹמֹה, and the name of a place, גִּלֹה, Josh. xv. 51; also אֲבַדֹּה, Prov. xxvii. 20, is the indication of Hades as a proper name, hence it cannot be translated, as Kurtz maintains, as an appelative: until he (Judah) comes to rest. We might rather consider שִׁילֹה, like שְׁלֹמֹה, as the name of a person, so that the Messiah can be called the bodily שַׁלְוָה (Ps. cxxii. 7), as the One in Himself full of rest, and as the One producing rest from Himself. This view commends itself not a little, and we could consider the prediction as a prediction concerning Solomon,—like the Samaritan translator of the Pentateuch into Arabic,—and beyond Solomon of his antitype. But vers. 11, 12 contradict this view, for in them Judah is the subject; the images appertain to the tribe which comes to Shiloh, and which rests from conflict in peace, not to the person of a single prince of peace.

Remark 3. — The polemic against the Jews has carried on a traditional misuse, which extends back to Justin's *Dialogue with Trypho*. According to this prophecy the subjugation of the Jewish people under heathen dominion is regarded as a preliminary sign of

the coming of the Messiah; and the conclusion is
drawn that since the people is in exile (אֵין מֶלֶךְ וְאֵין שָׂר,
"without a prince and without a king," Hos. iii. 4),
the Messiah must have come long since. This
explanation of the prophecy is even for this reason
inadmissible, because the prediction in this blessing,
that Judah should at length lose dominion, would
bring a gloom for which there would be no occasion.
Isaac Troki, in his חזוק אמונה, i. 14, is quite right,
where he contends against this interpretation with its
consequences. He is quite right when he maintains
that עד כִּי does not indicate that when the given
turning-point shall come Judah shall lose the
dominion, but that then Judah's dominion shall be
extended to world dominion (the so-called עד ועד בכלל,
see Levy, *Neuhebräisches Wörterbuch*, iii. 619^b); and
also because this interpretation is in contradiction
with the Christian faith, since Jesus sprung from
Judah, and is called the King of the Jews; and also
after He came the sceptre remained with the tribe of
Judah. But we do not agree with him in giving
מְקֹחֵק a personal interpretation, as in Deut. xxxiii. 21,
as referring to the legislators, to those who handle the
law, the chiefs of the people, which involves our
understanding מִבֵּין רַגְלָיו in the indecent signification
of Deut. xxviii. 57; nor do we agree with him
when he combines שִׁילֹה with שִׁלְיָה in the same
passage of Deuteronomy, and, according to the
Targum of Onkelos on this passage, understands
זְעֵר בְּנָהָא of the youngest, that is, of the final Son
of Judah, while שִׁלְיָה has also through the Mishna,
Talmud, and Syriac, rather the assured signification
of after-birth (*secundinae*). But in the main point

EXPLANATIONS OF SHILOH.

he is quite right, that according to the prophecy concerning Shiloh the kingdom of God from Judah, through the Messiah, will overcome all the kingdoms of this world, hence that the dominion of Judah without diminution will become extended to world dominion.

Remark 4.—Kurtz rejects the personal interpretation of שִׁילֹה for this reason, because the promise of a king, and, indeed, of one ruling the world, hence of the Messiah, here at the end of the patriarchal period is an anachronism. And, indeed, although along with the prediction concerning the blessing of the people in the seed of the patriarchs the prediction is connected, that the patriarchs shall be tribal ancestors of many peoples, and kings of peoples (Gen. xvii. 6, 16, xxxv. 11), the preliminary conditions for the future image of a king of Israel are not yet in existence: the tribes of Israel are only first in process of becoming a people; the theocratic relation of God begins first with the legislation, and the patriarchal house is not yet involved in wars, which press for a demand for one leadership. It is true that the promise respecting Judah has a royal sound; for שֵׁבֶט is the usual designation of honour for a king, but it does not have to do with a person, but with a tribe, and in such a way that from the standpoint of the further development, and especially of the fulfilment, one is the goal. As in the protevangel הוּא is mankind, and one is the centre; as in the promise concerning the blessing on the peoples בְּזַרְעֲךָ is the family of the patriarchs, and one is the centre: so here יְהוּדָה is the tribe, and one is the centre. If we compare the prophecy concerning Shiloh with the protevangel there appears to be rather retrogression than progression, but it is only apparent. The proclamation of salvation in its beginning was with reference to victory over the evil, and this beginning is the impelling germ of the following development until its utmost limit. A blessing on the nations is the contents of the proclamation of salvation in its second stage,—the development goes forward from this point, but departing from the all-comprehensive ideal placed in the beginning, as the plant, before it attains its ultimate end in the fruit which is preformed in germ, goes out in root, stem, and branches. The nationalizing of the proclamation of salvation is the root through which it is fastened, and the trunk which is to bear the fruit. With the blessing of Judah the nationalizing begins, after the way has already been prepared through the promise of the blessing of the nations in the seed of the patriarchs.

CHAPTER III.

THE PREDICTIONS OF THE MOSAIC PERIOD CONCERNING THE FUTURE SALVATION.

§ 10. *The Promise of a Prophet after Moses, and like him.*

THE future mediator of salvation appears later on as king, who as the chosen of Yahweh reigns over Israel, and from Israel over the nations. The prophecy of Shiloh is like the frame, which the later image of the Messiah fills out. But before we meet with a proper Messianic prophecy, there is given because of a special occasion, without connection with the expectation of an ideal king, the promise of a prophet like Moses. As the people at the giving of the Sinaitic law could not bear to hear the voice of Yahweh, on account of its dreadful nearness, and accordingly Moses must act as mediator (Deut. v. 23–28; cf. Ex. xx. 19), Yahweh promised the people for the future a prophet, who should be raised from their midst like Moses, and demanded for him in advance unconditional obedience (Deut. xviii. 15–19). [This is] an appendix to the history of the legislation, which is to be inserted after Deut.

v. 28, which is connected with the command not to make use of idolatrous means of witchcraft (Deut. xviii. 9-14), and which is completed in the indication of the signs through which a true is to be distinguished from a false prophet (Deut. xviii. 20 ff.).

In order that we may not be led to take a position against the individual and personal interpretation of the prophet who is promised, through the connection in which the prophecy concerning the prophet like Moses stands, we have to consider: (1) Moses is, according to the view of the Torah, the incomparable prophet. The true character of his personality in redemptive history proceeds from his prophetic calling, from which the legislative is never specially distinguished. Hence the unique character of the intimate relation of God with this His servant (Num. xii. 6-8) is compared with God's usual relations with the prophets, and he is called, as the one who is incomparable, by his proper official name נָבִיא (Deut. xxxiv. 10; cf. Hos. xii. 14). (2) Moses is, according to the history as it is given us in the Torah, not the only prophet of his time. His sister also bears the designation of prophetess, נְבִיאָה (Ex. xv. 20). Miriam and Aaron are conscious that God also speaks through them as well as through Moses (Num. xii. 2). The seventy elders, whom Moses appoints as his assistants, have a part of the Spirit of God which rests on him, and begin to prophesy, and the prophetic ecstasy seizes others also among the people (Num. xi. 24, 29), —there were also prophets at that time besides Moses, and the Torah presupposes that there always have been, and always will be prophets (Deut. xiii. 1 ff.). When, therefore, looking through forty years back to the first year it is promised (Deut. xviii. 15): "Yahweh thy God will raise out of the midst of thy brethren a prophet like me (כָּמֹנִי); unto him shall ye hearken," and ver. 18: "a prophet will I raise up to you out of the midst of thy brethren, like thee (כָּמוֹךָ)," the point of the prediction lies in the כָּמֹנִי and כָּמוֹךָ. The sense is not that God will always raise up a prophet to the people (Rosenmüller: *semper per futura tempora*), who, like Moses, will be His organ. It is exactly the emphasis on the continuation which is lacking. The imperfect יָקִים (אָקִים) is not an adequate expression for "always." Moreover, נָבִיא cannot be understood as a plural, for the singular is retained throughout, without being exchanged with the plural. The prophecy indicates a definite prophet, it indicates a single person; and the history of the following period confirms the [view], that the characteristic marks of the one in contradistinction to the many, which the concluding section (Deut. xviii. 20 ff.) presupposes, are involved in the כָּמֹנִי and כָּמוֹךָ. For all the prophets who followed Moses are not mediators of such a revelation as the Sinaitic; but the divine revelation which is like the Sinaitic lies for all in the domain of the future, and their duty consists in representing the spirit of the Sinaitic divine revelation, and thus preparing the way for a future divine revelation, whose mediator is to be the predicted prophet like

62 MESSIANIC PROPHECIES IN HISTORICAL SUCCESSION.

Moses! Only so understood is Deut. xviii. 15-19 justified as a part of the prophetic words which are to be discussed by us in historical succession. If the prediction only referred to the continuance of prophetic mediation in general, it would be without any Christological significance, for it would not contain any indication that the prophetic office after Moses would culminate in One, who would be greater than all the preceding. But the use of the singular, as has been pointed out, shows that not a succession of prophets is intended, but one prophet, who stands before the spirit of the speaker; and as the expressions בְּמֹנִי and כָּמוֹךָ demand, such an One, who is not only a continuation, but also an antitype of the mediatorship of Moses. That the future will not be without prophets is presupposed in the Torah, and not only especially promised, but it is promised that among these prophets there will be another Moses. It remains undetermined whether this other Moses is to be hoped for in the nearer or more remote future. The prediction brings that which is separated near together, and flies away over that which lies between the now and the coming time, which is separated perhaps by a gulf of more than a thousand years.

Remark 1.—Our interpretation of this passage gives again the impression which it makes on us, but we are not so daring as to attribute to the grounds of probability in its favour a compulsory power of proof. The impression which it makes on interpreters like Hävernick, Hofmann, Gustav Baur, Eduard König,

THE PROPHET LIKE MOSES.

von Orelli, Dillmann, and others is just the opposite. These interpreters contend against the reference to a single definite prophet, and find only one thought expressed, that God will raise up a mediator for His people, such as it now has in Moses, as often as it needs a mediator of a divine revelation. By the expression נָבִיא כָּמֹנִי we are not to understand a prophet who stands on the same plane with Moses; it indicates only one who is to be an organ of God like him, since here Moses and the other prophets are not compared as in Deut. xxxiv. 10, but Moses and the prophets like him as organs of God are compared with the heathen sorcerers. Hofmann says,[1] the singular is indeed not a collective, but is used with relation to the single case where the people need a mediator of the divine revelation. He also understands כָּמֹנִי (כָּמוֹךָ) in connection with (מִקֶּרֶב אֲחֵיהֶם) מִקִּרְבְּךָ מֵאַחֶיךָ, which stands by it, as meaning a prophet who like Moses is one of the people, which has this in its favour, since the warning against heathen sorcerers precedes. Among Jewish interpreters the reference to prophets after the time of Moses in a general sense predominates. But Aben Ezra is doubtful, and considers it possible that Joshua is intended. That was also the view of a part of the Samaritans.[2] The passage is used in the same way in the *Assumptio Mosis*, i. 5–7. In Jalkut the view is also maintained, that Jeremiah may be the One promised.

Remark 2.—It is a weighty reason against the single personal and eschatological interpretation of נָבִיא, that we never find in the canonical Scriptures

---

[1] *Schriftbeweis*, vol. ii. part 1, pp. 138–142.
[2] See the citations from Photius in Lightfoot on John iv. 19.

of the Old Testament an echo of this promise. On the other hand, if in the pre-Christian and apostolic age this interpretation was adopted to a considerable extent, it must yet have had a tradition for it reaching back we do not know how far. Among the Samaritans, whose canon consists exclusively of the five books of Moses, Deut. xviii. 15, 18 was regarded as the only proper Messianic prophecy. The word of the Samaritan woman, John iv. 25: "I know that Messiah comes: when He shall come He will declare unto us all things," shows that the Messiah was represented as a mediator of salvation. A Samaritan, whose name was Dositheus,[1] who claimed to be the Messiah, maintained that he was therefore the prophet who was promised in Deut. xviii. But also in the New Testament Scriptures this passage is considered as a *locus illustris* of eschatological meaning, as a prophecy which has come to its realization in Jesus Christ. In the address of Peter, which was made in the porch of Solomon, the prophet who is predicted by Moses is compared with the prophets who have prepared the way for his coming since Samuel (Acts iii. 22-24). And Stephen, presupposing the meaning of the passage as referring to Christ, emphasizes Deut. xviii. 15 as one of the most significant words of Moses (Acts vii. 37). When Philip says to Nathanael (John i. 45): "We have found Him of whom Moses in the law did write," there is nothing fitter there, as well as in John v. 46, than to think of this prophecy of the future prophet. We are led with probability to conclude that this interpretation of the passage was not isolated, since

[1] Uhlhorn in Herzog and Plitt's *Real-Encyklopädie für protestantische Theologie und Kirche*, Leipzig 1878, vol. iii. p. 683.

also the expectation of the people in the time of Christ was directed to a great prophet who was absolutely called ὁ προφήτης (John vi. 14). But how this prophet was related to the Messiah was not clear. The people distinguished both (John i. 19-21, vii. 40-42), although in the face of Jesus Christ the perception of the oneness of the prophet and of the Messiah disappeared (Matt. xxi. 9—11).

§ 11. *The Prophecy of Balaam concerning the Star and the Sceptre out of Israel.*

It is related in the grandiloquent parasha (section) of Balak, in Numbers (xxii. 2 and elsewhere), that Balak, king of the Moabites, when the kingdoms of Sihon and Og became subject to the military prowess of Israel, summoned the celebrated Balaam of Pethor, north-east of Aleppo, in order that he might utter a curse against the people who were pressing forward so victoriously; but that, overcome by the Spirit of Yahweh, in spite of all Balak's efforts, he blessed Israel and prophesied their glorious future. This is an event which also, outside of that parasha, is celebrated as an integral part of the miracles of the Exodus (Deut. xxiii. 5 f.; Josh. xxiv. 9 f.; Micah vi. 5; Neh. xiii. 2).

We admit that the narrative, as it lies before us, is combined out of several sources that may be clearly distinguished, and that the historical element, as it survived in the " sage," has been reproduced, not without literary co-operation, but without doubting the fact that the heathen sorcerer, contrary to his natural disposition, became a prophet of Yahweh, and that he received an insight into the future of Israel, whose significance only has its counterpart in the second part of the Book of Zechariah and the Book of Daniel.

As Balaam reached Moab, especially the district above the Arnon, which Sihon, who was now conquered by Israel, had snatched from the Moabites, Balak shows him three times a place from which he has a view of Israel (Num. xxii. 41, xxiii. 14, 28). He brings great offerings in order, if possible, to secure the compliance of Yahweh; but Balaam must, in spite of these, bless instead of curse. This takes place in three predictive utterances, which are joined on to the three-[fold] setting up [of altars] (Num. xxiii. 7–10, 18–24, xxiv. 3–9). Finally, giving up signs, he submits to the will of God, which he now recognises as unchangeable, and unveils to the king, as he departs from him, the future in four great predictive utterances: concerning the great king out of Israel (xxiv. 15–19), destruction of Amalek (ver. 20), captivity of the Kenites through Asshur (ver. 21 f.), destruction of the world power out of the west (ver. 33 f., cf. on צִים מִיַּד כִּתִּים, 1 Macc. i. 1, viii. 5; Dan. xi. 30). It is characteristic in connection with the political element of the older announcement of the Messiah that we receive the first prophecy of this kind within the course of Old Testament history from the mouth of a heathen seer. The fourth of the seven מְשָׁלִים of Balaam, introduced through ver. 14—" And now, behold I go unto my people: come, permit thyself to be reminded of

BALAAM'S PROPHECY ABOUT THE STAR. 67

what this people shall do to thy people in the course of the days "—is as follows :—

15 Utterance of Balaam the son of Beôr,
And utterance of the man with punctured [1] eyes.

16 Utterance of the perceiver of divine words,
And of the knower of the knowledge of the Most High,
Who sees visions of the Almighty,
Sunk down and with eyes unveiled.

17 I see him, though not yet ;
I behold him, though not near.
There comes forth a star out of Jacob,
And rises a sceptre out of Israel,
And dashes in pieces the flanks of Moab,
And tears to the ground all the sons of Sheth ; [2]
And Edom shall be a conquest,
Yea Seir, his enemy, shall be a conquest,
And Israel retains the victory.

19 And he rules from Jacob,
And destroys those who have escaped from [hostile] cities." [3]

---

[1] [German : *Aufgestochenen Auges*, Latin of the ed. of 1880, *perforatus oculo*.]—C.

[2] Thus we translate with the Septuagint and Jerome, but without understanding who or what is meant by Sheth (שֵׁת). Jer. xlviii. 45 transforms בְּנֵי שֵׁת into בְּנֵי שָׁאוֹן, "sons of the tumult of war ;" perhaps he understands שֵׁת in the sense of שְׁאֵת, Lam. iii. 47, from שָׁאָה, to roar, to make a desolate noise. We might also choose the reading שְׂאֵת=שֵׁת, elevation, pride, which gives an admirable meaning ; for a characteristic trait of Moab is pride, as that of Edom the hatred of heirs, so that Zunz translates : "All the sons of boasting." The Pilpel קרקר, according to post-biblical literature (see Levy, *Neuhebräisches Wörterbuch*, iv. p. 391), certainly signifies to rend, to tear down, and this can also be said of persons in an objective way, just as much as הָפַךְ, Prov. xii. 7, and הָרַס. Ex. xv. 7 ; Ps. xxviii. 5 ; Jer. xlii. 10.

[3] As in Num. xxiv. 9*b*, Gen. xxvii. 29 is repeated, and in Num. xxiii. 24, xxiv. 9*a*, Gen. xlix. 9, so here 19*b* reminds us of Gen. xxii. 17*b*.

Here first the object of the Old Testament hope is personified, for star and sceptre are images of a ruler who, like a star, appears out of Israel, a ruler of earthly extraction and heavenly splendour. Before the eye of the seer there stands in the distant future a king who is to be expected, who subjugates Moab and Edom, and makes Israel a victorious, powerful people. That which the last three predictions express concerning Amalek, Kain (the Kenites), and the world powers of the East (Asshur) and of the West (ships from the coast of Kittim), has no connection with this king. It is not said that the downfall of these peoples and kingdoms will be mediated through him. Since only the subjugation of the Moabites and Edomites is expressly imputed to him, that which is predicted does not rise beyond that which was accomplished by Saul (1 Sam. xiv. 47), and more permanently by David (2 Sam. viii.). Nevertheless the subjugation through David was only a temporary one; hence Jeremiah, in chaps. xlviii., xlix., again takes up Balaam's prophetic words concerning Moab and Edom, and places them in the future. And that which is said in ver. 19 is indefinite, and is understood in the Messianic echoes of Ps. lxxii. 8, Zech. ix. 10, in an absolute sense. But in order to understand this prophecy as one which is to have a New Testament fulfilment, we must remove its kernel, which consists in this, that the Messiah will subjugate the world through the power of the Spirit, and, scourging, will subdue those who oppose Him;—thus understood, the ultimate fulfilment of that which is prophesied yet belongs to the future. But in every case where an empire like the old Roman world empire gives up its national gods, and acknowledges the God who has revealed Himself in Christ, Christianity celebrates a victory over the world; and when this shall once lie at the feet of the Lord and of the Christ who is enthroned at His right hand, then the dominion of the Messiah out of Jacob, and the completion of His punishment on those who contend against Him, will be ultimately fulfilled spiritually, but not only inwardly, also externally, but not in a military way.

Remark.—Also in the New Testament the star is a Messianic emblem and attribute. The Oriental magi say (Matt. ii. 2): "We have seen His star;" and He calls himself, Rev. xxii. 16, the radiant morning star." Rabbi Akiba called that Simeon who placed himself at the head of the national rising under Hadrian, with reference to Num. xxiv. 17, *as* the King Messiah, the son of the star (בר כוכבא). On the contrary, that which is said in Rev. xii. 5 concerning the Messiah, who is born out of Israel, with the iron sceptre, does not refer immediately to Num. xxiv. 17, but to Ps. ii. 8 f.

§ 12. *Course and Goal of the History of Salvation, after Moses' great Memorial Song.*

The two pentateuchal songs, Ex. xv. and Deut. xxxii., each stand in its way in a closer relation to the further development of the proclamation of redemption. When Balaam, before his spiritual eyes discern the ideal human king of Israel, celebrates God Himself as the king of this people (Num. xxiii. 21*b*, xxiv. 7*b*), this takes place because of the theocratic relation which dates from the Sinaitic legislation, for their Yahweh was king in Jeshurun, as is said in Deut. xxxiii. 5, from the standpoint of the forty years of the exodus ; and the hymn which rung out in the year of the exodus, after the deliverance through the Red Sea, closes with the words, which are to be regarded as a fundamental part of the song, which was enlarged in the mouths of the post-Mosaic congregation (Ex. xv. 58), " Yahweh shall be king for ever and ever." This kingdom of Yahweh is the presupposition of the Messianic kingdom, the basis of the kingdom of the promise. And Moses' testamentary song, although it speaks only concerning the God of salvation, and not the mediator of salvation, is nevertheless like a chart of the ways of God, an outline of the stations of the history of redemption, into which later disclosures concerning the human mediation of the redemption are to be introduced. Summoning heaven and earth as witnesses of his proclamation, the poet takes his stand in the midst of the time, when Israel, borne by Yahweh his Creator on eagle's wings through the wilderness to the land overflowing with milk and honey, and there blessed with the richest abundance of temporal benefits, in fleshly arrogance and contemptuous unthankfulness rewards his God and Father with apostasy to the idols of the heathen. At this time this song proclaims to them the word of God. The word וַיֹּאמֶר (" and he said ") introduces the divine discourse, to which the mouth of testimony is to be opened. Israel, because of his apostasy, is to be brought through God's judgments to the brink of destruction. But now, in the midst of the threatened punishment, there is the budding comfort, that the honour of Yahweh in respect to Israel's enemies does not suffer the punishment to proceed to complete overthrow. He makes use of the heathen as instruments of punishment against His people; but after He has shown Himself against them as a strict judge, and after He has destroyed the apostate mass, He manifests Himself as a pitier and avenger of His servants, and the result of Israel's history is finally this, that God's people, sifted and expiated, again inhabit their native land, and that all peoples unite in praising God who has revealed Himself in judgment and grace.

The shout, הַרְנִינוּ גוֹיִם עַמּוֹ, admits of two explanations: "Break forth in rejoicing, peoples, his people," which is an asyndeton, as there immediately follows in עַדְכְּתוֹ עַמּוֹ a similar, although less hard, expression, —or, "ye peoples cause his people to rejoice." In the latter case הרנין has an objective accusative, like רִנֶּן (Ps. li. 16, lix. 17).[1] The thought remains the same, for the rejoicing in both cases has reference to God, who in the history of Israel shows Himself to be the living and holy One, who, after He has punished

[1] The Targum also wavers: Onkelos and the first Jerusalem consider הרנינו as transitive; the second Jerusalem—where we are to read קלסו קדמוהי עממיא, not עמא—consider עמו, like גוים, as in the vocative.

His apostate people, does not proceed to extremes, but again has compassion on those who finally serve Him, and avenges the blood of His servants. It is, in reality, the same conclusion as that which is reached in chaps. x. and xi. of the Epistle to the Romans: "God hath shut up all under unbelief, that He might have mercy upon all." The apostle, too, shows there how the history of redemption in intricate ways reaches a glorious result, and concludes with a song of praise to the all-compassionate God (Rom. xi. 32 ff.). Modern criticism, indeed, denies that the great song, Deut. xxxii., was composed by Moses; but it contains nothing which betrays a post-Mosaic origin, for אַפְאֵיהֶם (ver. 26a) does not refer to an exiling, but to an annulling; and an abundance of evident connections with the Book of the Covenant (Ex. xix.–xxiv.), with the blessing of Moses (Deut. xxxiii.), and with the Tefilla Moses (Ps. xc.), prevent us from holding that the testimony of Deut. xxxi. 22 is self-deception, or deception for a purpose (*tendentiöse Täuschung*); and it can be more easily conceived that the legislation is not indicated in it with a single word—for יְבוֹנְנֵהוּ (ver. 10b) does not signify *erudivit eum*—when the legislator is the speaker, whose poetic gift is attested through such highly poetical words as Ex. xvii. 16, Num. x. 35 f., than when a later poet who has put himself in the spirit of Moses is the speaker.[1]

---

[1] See concerning the Song of Moses my *Pentateuch-kritischen Studien*, x. *Die Entstehung des Deuteronomiums, Zeitschrift für Kirchliche Wissenschaft und Kirchliches Leben*, Leipzig 1880, pp. 505–508.

Remark 1.—In harmony with its high antiquity, the song does not exhibit any strophical form. In four pictures it describes the history of Israel until its completion: first, Israel's creation and gracious preferment, vers. 1–14; then Israel's unthankfulness and apostasy, vers. 15–19; then God's punitive judgments, vers. 20–34; and, finally, when Israel's foot totters, and he is near the brink, the revenge and retribution against his enemies and those of his God, vers. 35–43. It is significant here that the people which experiences this vengeance, new life, and healing, is called עֲבָדָיו, vers. 36*a*, 43*a*. In its apostasy it is called לֹא בָנָיו מוּמָם, "not his children, a shame to themselves" (5*a*, cf. Prov. ix. 7); the turning from wrath to mercy has reference to the people who are brought again from their apostasy, and who no longer serve strange gods, but the God whom they had forgotten (vers. 15–18).

Remark 2.—It is indicated that Israel will draw the heathen to a common worship of their God in the benedictions of Moses concerning the heathen territory bordering on the northern tribes of Zebulon and Issachar, when it is said (Deut. xxxiii. 18 f.): "They will call peoples to the mountain [the place where Yahweh is worshipped]; there they will sacrifice sacrifices of righteousness." The word עַמִּים is not to be understood here as in ver. 3 of the tribes of Israel; and הַר probably does not have another meaning than in Ex. xv. 17.

CHAPTER IV.

THE MESSIANIC PROPHECIES OF THE TIME OF JOSHUA AND OF THE JUDGES.

§ 13. *Yahweh and His Anointed in the Thanksgiving Song of Hannah.*

THE great song of Moses really treats of the changing relation of Israel to his God, without there being an occasion to mention a divinely-anointed One; but the Mosaic law of the king (Deut. xvii. 14 ff.) shows how near the thought of a king was immediately before the conquest of Canaan. The peoples with whom Israel had to do were all under a monarchial form of government.[1] The royal rule which the legislation had in view, and for which it had prudently given rules, became in the time of the Judges an object of longing and hope. The song, 1 Sam. ii. 1–10, in which Hannah in Shiloh, as a richly blessed mother, after long disgrace, praises the Lord, closes with words which show how the people, during the torn condition of the popular bond at that time and of heathen

[1] See concerning the law of the king, *Der Gesetzkodex des Deuteronomiums. Zeitschrift für Kirchliche Wissenschaft, u.s.w.*, Leipzig 1880, pp. 559–567.

degeneration, comforted themselves with the future prospect of a united royal government:

> 10 Yahweh, His adversaries shall be broken in pieces,
> It thunders before Him in heaven—
> Yahweh will judge the ends of the earth,
> And will grant power to His king,
> And will exalt the horn of His anointed.

We do not deny the possibility that the song, without being composed by Hannah, may only have been assigned to her by a historian; but we deny decidedly that it does not harmonize with her position and feelings, and that therefore it could not be composed by her. She sees in her elevation from disgrace to honour the wonderful power of God, which humbles the high and exalts the lowly; for that is the manner of the true poet, to idealize his experiences, that is, to place them under a universal point of view, and to behold the great in the small, the whole in the individual, the essential in the accidental. And why should not Hannah, who had borne Samuel under her heart, the founder of the school of the prophets, who anointed David the sweet singer of Israel, not have possessed the gift of poetry?[1] Or are we to think of

[1] Klostermann calls this song merely one speaking out of the soul of Hannah, but not a psalm composed by her. A dictatorial assumption of that which cannot be proved! This song, like all old songs, is not strophical; but he forces upon it a form of composition in tetrastichs, and concludes from this arbitrary presupposition that the last two lines (ver. 10*b*) must be a later addition, after the example of Ps. xxix. 11. Moreover, the song pleases us in the traditional text far better than in his wild corrected one, as, *e.g.*, ver. 10: "It is Yahweh who frightens

David in the mention which is made of the divinely-anointed one, so that the close of the song expresses a hope out of David's age assigned to the time of the Judges, and which therefore excludes Hannah's authorship? But the true state of the case is this, that the anointed of God who is hoped for is neither David nor an ultimate Messiah after the conclusion of a long series of kings; rather there stands before the soul of the poetess an ideal king whom Yahweh has appointed, and through whom He brings His cause to victory. We have to do here with the casting down of the enemies of Yahweh from one end of the earth to another, and with the raising up of the Messianic kingdom, or, as we can say without introducing anything which does not belong there, with the raising up of the kingdom of God in His Christ, after the thunder and lightning of divine judgment have made way for this kingdom. The political use of power, which concerns the preservation and elevation of the nation, attain here to an ethical inwardness, which does not appear in Balaam's prophecy.

§ 14. *The divinely-anointed One in the Threatening Prophecy concerning the House of Eli.*

The prophecy in 1 Sam. ii. 27–36 shows how anxiously the period of the Judges looked after a

away His enemies, He who rides on high in heaven and thunders. Cf. on עָלָיו in his commentary on Ps. xlii., and in mine. We cannot decide whether יַרְעֵם is considered active: "He thunders," or impersonal: "it thunders."

future king of Israel, in which an unknown אִישׁ אֱלֹהִים [man of God] announces to Eli and his house the loss of all previous high-priestly dignity and all sorts of punishment without absolutely denying to the members of this house entrance to the priestly service. This prophecy in connection with 1 Kings ii. 27, 35 and Ezek. xliv. is a main prop for the degradation of the Elohistic Torah, or the so-called Priests' Code, into the post-exilic period, since it is thought that this prophecy, which is assigned from the post-Deuteronomic standpoint to the time of the Judges, deprives the entire Aaronic original house of Eli of the priestly prerogatives, and prepares the transition to Zadok, an upstart from an unknown race. Indeed the prophecy sounds as if not only the house of Eli, which, as appears from 1 Chron. xxiv. 3, 5, was derived from Ithamar, the second son of Aaron, but as if his entire priestly patriarchal house, was to be destroyed. But [the assumption] that Zadok was not a Levite contradicts the sense of the Old Testament Scriptures in all their parts, hence it is emphasized as one of the illegal acts of Jeroboam (1 Kings xii. 31), that he even appointed priests who were not Levites; and there is not adequate ground for holding that the genealogical tracing of Zadok back to Eleazar, the first-born of Aaron, by the chronicler (1 Chron. v. 30–34, vi. 35–38, xxiv. 3, cf. xxvii. 17; Ezra vii. i. f.), is designed to be a concealment of his obscure origin. The true state of the case is therefore this, that in ver. 27 the patriarchal house of Eli is regarded as the same with the priestly house of Levi, chosen since the exodus from Egypt in the person of Aaron, and those descendants of Aaron are excluded from the promise of a constant official service before God made to the entire priestly house of Levi, who do not honour the Lord through their walk, but who dishonour Him. This concerns, however, the present priestly house of the line of Ithamar. This line is threatened with deep degradation and with the transition of the high-priestly office, whose insignia is the wearing of the ephod, to a better priest than Eli. This better priest, according to ver. 34 f., seems to belong to the immediate future; but the prophecy was fulfilled only gradually, and not in its entire severity.

Abiathar, the son of Ahimelech, who, as Saul caused the priests in Nob to be assassinated, escaped with the ephod to David, and shared with him the troubles of the time of persecution (1 Sam. ii. 20 and further), is the last high priest of the line of Ithamar. He it was who, for the benefit of Adonijah, had entered into the conspiracy against Solomon, and was therefore deposed by Solomon and banished to Anathoth, which, according to 1 Kings ii. 27, was regarded as a fulfilment of the divine word which went forth against the house of Eli. But, according to 1 Sam. xiv. 3, Ahijah, a grandson of Eli, still wore the high-priestly ephod in Shiloh; later according to 1 Sam. xxi. 2, xxii. 9 ff., Ahijah's brother, Ahimelech, served in Nob and made known the divine will, and also that Abiathar, who escaped from the massacre by Saul, and who along with Zadok remained true to David in the persecution of Absalom (2 Sam. xv. 24, xvii. 15), is still named under Solomon as priest (1 Kings iv. 4) along with Zadok, although in the second place.

The threatening prediction, therefore, concerning the house of Eli, has not at all the appearance of a fiction; it also has in the two difficult passages with מָעוֹן (1 Sam. ii. 29a, 32a) the stamp of ancient tradition.[1] According to this, we are not to think that it is Solomon who is intended, when it is said in ver. 35: "And I will raise me up a faithful priest, that shall do according to that which is in my heart and in my mind; and I will build him a permanent house; and he shall walk before my anointed (לִפְנֵי־מְשִׁיחִי) for ever." If this is really a divinely-granted glimpse into the future, we are obliged to recognise its ideal character without looking at the historical details. It pertains to a priest after God's heart, and to a king after God's heart, and to a lasting unbroken co-operation of both, and contains an actual proof that the hope of the believers toward the end of the period of the Judges was directed to a king, to be realized according to the theocratic idea, *to* a Messiah ($X\rho\iota\sigma\tau\acute{o}s$) of God.

[1] It remains ever most probable that in 29a מָעוֹן is the accusative of relation, and in 32a צַר מָעוֹן signifies the "distress of the dwelling of God" (cf. צַר רוּחִי, Job vii. 11. See Keil). The Septuagint reads in 29a, כְּעַיִן ($\dot{a}\nu\alpha\iota\delta\epsilon\tilde{\iota}\ \dot{o}\phi\theta\alpha\lambda\mu\tilde{\omega}$), which involves the transmutation of תִּבְעֲטוּ into the contradictory תבעט, and it leaves 32a entirely untranslated.

CHAPTER V.

PROPHECY AND CHOKMA IN THE AGE OF DAVID AND SOLOMON.

§ 15. *The Transition of the Kingdom from Benjamin to Judah.*

SAMUEL, the late-born son of Hannah, whom she dedicated to the service of Yahweh in Shiloh, is the new founder of the order of the prophets (Acts iii. 24), and the founder of the kingdom. It is due to him that the barbarism of the period of the Judges is followed by the golden age of the history and literature of Israel. The period of Saul, the king from the tribe of Benjamin, forms only the transition to it. His kingdom was only preliminary, and proved itself to be a failure. His presumptuous action in one of his last wars decided his dethronement. In that great utterance (1 Sam. xv. 22 f.) which became the watchword of later prophecy and psalmody, Samuel announced it to him.[1] Without associating any more with the

[1] It is as follows: "Has Yahweh as great delight in burnt-offerings and sacrifices as in obeying the voice of Yahweh? Behold, to obey is better than sacrifice, and to hearken than the fat of rams; for rebellion is the sin of witchcraft, and wilfulness is idolatry and teraphim worship."

king he withdrew to Rama (1 Sam. xv. 34 f.). Thence he was sent with the anointing horn to the house of Jesse. There in the seminary of the prophets at Nayoth flourished under his leadership prophecy and music (2 Kings iii. 15), the spiritual powers which should glorify the coming kingdom of promise. There, in the unapproachable retreat of the Spirit's activity, the future king concealed himself by the side of Samuel from the fury of the present one. There Saul himself also, as in the beginning of his kingdom (1 Sam. x. 10) so now in its decline, was seized by the irresistible power of the prophetic Spirit (1 Sam. xix. 23 f.), whose activity is likewise called הִתְנַבֵּא, as (1 Sam. xviii. 10) the violent ecstatic behaviour into which the spirit of melancholy and jealousy transported him. In a case where one who is seized by the prophetic Spirit is ethically unlike it, as Balaam and Saul, the strong chain through which the spirit and flesh are bound needs to be overcome and broken. Saul was indeed the anointed of Yahweh, and as long as he lived was considered even by David an inviolable person (2 Sam. i. 14). From time to time his better self broke through the gloom of the malice and melancholy with which he was enshrouded. But he never raised himself to an ideally theocratic conception of his royal office. This begins first with David, through whom, since the free agency of Saul and God's decree were combined (cf. 1 Sam. xiii. 13), the sceptre passed over to Judah.

§ 16. *David's View of Himself after his Anointing.*

After the removal of the Benjaminitish kingdom all the expectations of salvation, with which the believers of Israel looked into the future, were centred on the new kingdom which was in process of development, and David himself, after receiving the charismatic chrism, must have appeared to himself all the more significant for the history of salvation, in proportion as he was more joyfully conscious of the fullest devotion to the divine ideal of his royal office. That which Judah, according to the blessing of Jacob, and the future king, according to the utterance of Balaam, should do for their people was indeed so slightly superhuman that David could well regard himself as the king predicted and hoped for. But the person of the theocratic king was even now so significant that David, through this Messianic view of himself, received a central and sacred significance which was of importance for the history of the world. That which the old patriarchal promise says concerning the seed of Abraham, that those who bless him should be blessed, and those that curse him should be cursed, David must now refer to himself. His enemies were considered by him as the enemies of Yahweh, and the imprecations which are hurled against them, even if they have more of an Old than a New Testament spirit, do not proceed from an egotism which overvalues itself. All his psalms are penetrated with the consciousness that his destiny and that of his

DAVID'S VIEW OF HIMSELF AFTER HIS ANOINTING. 83

enemies stands, according to the divine decree, in causal connection with the final result of human history; and since he places himself in the light of the Messianic ideal, he is wafted to an ideal height, where he is raised far above the accidental events of his life. This is the case in Ps. xvi. 9–11, where the hopes which he expresses go far beyond the thought that God this time—perhaps as he lay sick —would not suffer him to die. Viewing himself in the light of his exalted calling and of his intimate union with God as God's anointed and beloved (cf. ver. 10*b* with iv. 4, הִפְלָה ה' חָסִיד לוֹ), he expects for himself an endless life without falling into Hades, a continuous life with a heavenly perspective, in whose line without an end death is a vanishing element. He expects for himself that which was not fulfilled in him, but in the second David, and first through the second David was also mediately fulfilled in him. Speaking hyperbolically concerning himself, he became a prophet (Acts ii. 29–32).[1] The most striking example of this is in Ps. xxii. Neither in the life of David nor in the life of any Old Testament man of God can a situation be found which can make the deep

[1] In order properly to justify such explanations we must consider: (1) that the New Testament writings do not strictly discriminate between type and prophecy, but combine prediction in deed and word under the general designation of prophecy; (2) that it considers those things in the Psalms of David which transcend his actual experiences as predictions concerning the future Christ; and (3) that it regards the utterance of prophecy, not only with respect to its contents but also with regard to words, as the work of the Spirit mediated by man.

lamentations of this psalm over direct internal and external sufferings conceivable. Only perhaps what David experienced, according to 1 Sam. xxiii. 25 f., when pursued by Saul, could have given occasion to this psalm. But it is inconceivable that the distress in the wilderness of Maon could have corresponded to the remarkably cruel elements of suffering in this psalm. In it David speaks of himself as if he were the crucified Christ, whose rescue from deadly peril, narrated by himself, and from mouth to mouth, will be the consolation of all sufferers, and which will result in the conversion of the heathen, and in the setting up of the kingdom of God among mankind. David's and Christ's path through suffering to glory stand related as type and antitype. But the category of the type does not suffice for such a psalm as the twenty-second. In it the typical fact appears to be hyperbolically magnified beyond itself, and since this hyperbolical element corresponds exactly with the passion of Jesus Christ and its consequences, the spirit of prophecy is the impelling and formative element in these hyperbolical lamentations and views (1 Pet. i. 11).[1]

We must not, however, use the twenty-second Psalm for the history of the progressive Messianic

[1] If we presuppose that the speaker in the psalm is the poet, but that he transports himself into the position and mind of the suffering righteous man (Hengstenberg), or of the ideal Israel, the servant of Yahweh (Cheyne), the state of the case is psychologically the same. But if we granted that the poet made some one else than himself the speaker, the psalm would be without a parallel.

proclamation. The fifty-third chapter of Isaiah first gives us the key to this psalm, which, however, we may judge regarding the poet, and the time in which the poet lived and the person of the one described, remains a spiritual prodigy, and can first be understood in the light of New Testament fulfilment. For the history which prophesies in types is the image of God, before which beginning, middle, and end are alike eternally present; but the revelation of God, even that which the types set forth, is defined and measured pedagogically according to the ever recurring historical position and stage of its respective period.

17. *The Binding of the Promise to the House of David.*

It was not in the time soon after the carrying of the Ark of the Covenant home to Zion, as might appear from the connection of the narrative (2 Sam. vi., vii.), but much later in the period, after the victorious wars[1] related in chaps. v. and viii., and before the birth of Solomon (cf. 2 Sam. vii. 12 with 1 Chron. xxii. 9), that David formed the purpose of building Yahweh a temple, which, as Nathan the prophet reveals to him, Yahweh declines, but reserves the execution of the purpose for " his seed after him ; "

[1] The Ammonitish Syrian war, which lasted three years, can scarcely be included, for we can hardly suppose, with Köhler, vol. ii. p. 318 f., that his grievous sin with Bathsheba preceded the promises in chap. vii. instead of following them.

he responds, however, with the promise of the everlasting possession of the kingdom, so that even the sins of the descendants of David, which draw divine chastisement after them, cannot frustrate the divine pledge, as was the case with Saul.

According to this, that which Nathan announces to David extends to the entire course of history which follows through all futurity. It is true that the promise that David's seed should build the Lord a house (1 Chron. xxii. 7–10, xxviii. 10, xxix. 1) was applied by David to Solomon, and by Solomon to himself (1 Kings v. 19, viii. 17–20), but is later taken up by Zechariah (vi. 12) as yet to be fulfilled. The forty years' reign of Solomon is indeed only a brief part of the endless duration of the Davidic throne, indicated by עַד עוֹלָם (2 Sam. vii. 13). Also the promise in ver. 14: "I will be to him a father, and he shall be to me a son," does not apply exclusively to Solomon, nor in general to this or that ruler from the house of David, but to the Davidic rulers as such. But when it is further said that, in case David's posterity sin, God will chastise them with the stripes of men, without withdrawing His grace from the house of David and overthrowing the throne of David, that would be an assurance which would fall to the ground if, in spite of the breaking off of the Davidic royal line with Zedekiah, the throne of David had not proved to be continuous in the absolute person of the second David, who stood in a unique relation of a child to God, and who is introduced into the

PROMISE SECURED TO HOUSE OF DAVID. 87

world as heir of the throne of David his ancestor (Luke i. 32).

In his prayer of thanksgiving (2 Sam. vii. 18–29 and the parallel passage, 1 Chron. xvii. 16, 17) David sees in the fatherly relation in which God has placed Himself to his house a deep condescension, for he says: "Thou hast spoken to the house of Thy servant in the distant future, and, indeed, as is the law of men [the mode of dealing commanded], Yahweh, Almighty," that is, condescending to a relation, as is the divinely-ordered rule between father and son.[1] This deep condescension of God is, at the same time, David's highest exaltation. This is the turn which the Chronicler gives to David's words of praise, which are, according to 1 Chron. xvii. 17, "Thou hast regarded me according to the rank[2] of a man of station" (*hominis excelsitatis*, cf. the syntax of 1 Chron. xv. 27), *i.e.* of a man who is honoured with the highest exaltation (cf. הֻקַם עָל, 2 Sam. xxiii. 1). In Ps. xviii. 36 David compresses in two words, עֲנְוָתְךָ תַרְבֵּנִי, what he designs to say through the reciprocal relation of וְזֹאת וּרְאִיתַנִי כְּתוֹר הָאָדָם הַמַּעֲלָה and תּוֹרַת הָאָדָם, that is, Thy humility (condescension) hath made me great.

Remark.—It appears from the following considera-

[1] Joseph Rabinowitsch sees in this וְזֹאת תּוֹרַת הָאָדָם an indication of the Messianic Torah, which concerns mankind, in distinction from the national limited Sinaitic Torah.

[2] The word תּוֹר as in Esther signifies row, series, rank, according to which the Targum renders כתור by כסדר. If תּוֹר is taken as equivalent to תֹּאַר (cf. תּוֹרִיתָא, form, *Berachoth* 37b), the sense remains the same.

tions that Jesus was really the son of David:—(1) Those who sought help addressed Him as the son of David (Matt. ix. 27, xv. 22, xx. 30 f.; cf. Luke xviii. 38 f.; Mark x. 47 f.). (2) He was greeted by the people on His entrance into Jerusalem with "Hosanna to the son of David" (Matt. xxi. 9); and even by the children this cry was repeated (xxi. 15), without the scribes and Pharisees denying His right to this designation of honour. (3) Even, aside from the two genealogies, Joseph in Matthew (i. 20) as well as in Luke (i. 27) is indicated as a son of David, *i.e.* as springing from the house of David; for His genealogy, according to Jewish law, was reckoned, not after the mother, but after the father (משפחת אם אינה קרויה משפחה); in this case after Joseph, since Jesus was his legitimate son, because although not begotten by him, He was nevertheless born into his marriage relationship. (4) The apostles indicate Him, according to His human nature, as sprung from the seed of David (Rom. i. 3; 2 Tim. ii. 8; Rev. iii. 7, v. 5, xxii. 16). With regard to both genealogies, Luke is not concerned to show that Mary was a descendant of David, for he does not mention her name at the head of the genealogy. The right interpretation of ὡς ἐνομίζετο is given by Eusebius in the passage communicated by Credner:[1] There were among the Jews two kinds of opinions, since the Messiah on the one hand was derived from the line of David through Solomon, and on the other hand from the same line through Nathan, because through Jeremiah (xxii. 30) the royal succession was denied to that [line, *i.e.* of Solomon].[2] It is nevertheless

[1] Credner, *Einleitung in das Neue Testament*, p. 68 f.
[2] See No. 12 of my Talmudical Studies: "Die zweifache Genea-

possible that Mary also, as daughter of Eli (Luke iii. 23), was a descendant of David, and that Joseph, the son of Jacob, was brought up with her at the same time in the house of Eli, and married her.

§ 18. *The Separation of the Image of the Messiah from the Person of David.*

After those great promises had been uttered by Nathan to David which had the everlasting continuance of his throne, and therefore the inheritance of the kingdom within his house as their centre, his view of himself suffered at the same time a depression; for now he is no longer the chosen one divinely anointed, but the ancestor of a royal family, the first among an indefinite number, to whom after him the kingdom of the promise is to be transmitted. But the case is not so that in the series of rulers whom the promise has in prospect one who is pre-eminent above all others, or who closed the series, was placed before the soul of David; for that one would carry into execution David's purpose to build God a temple, does not imply in itself any pre-eminence over David. On the other hand we must suppose that David, when he measured himself by the theocratic ideal, must have indulged the hope that the government of one of his successors would succeed in an incomparably higher degree in realizing this ideal than had been the case with him; and as when, in the third year of the Ammonitish and

logie des Messias," *Zeitschrift für die lutherische Theologie und Kirche*, Leipzig 1860.

Syrian war, in the midst of the conquest of Rabbath Ammon, which brought the war to a close, as he found himself on the summit of external glory, he plunged into the twofold sin of adultery and murder, which, although he repented and obtained forgiveness, yet shadowed his life until the end, and brought him into a wrong position; from that time his Messianic view of himself must have suffered a tremendous shock, and his hope have been so much the more decidedly directed to a son exalted above himself, a Messiah of God in reality. This conclusion is confirmed by Ps. cx. If in this psalm David himself did not speak of one that was higher, but the people, or, as von Orelli thinks, a prophet (Nathan) concerning David, there would be no psalm at all in which the Messiah would occupy for David the position of a future person. The New Testament Scriptures, however, presuppose that David speaks in this psalm of another rather than of himself, that, as if he had descended from his throne, he bows himself before the One who is at the same time his Son and his Lord, and that therefore, so to speak, the type lays his crown at the feet of the antitype; and we know no counter proofs which compel us to correct[1] the view of the psalm, with which the argu-

[1] Jesus argues in this passage *e concessis*—an example for the fact that the religious knowledge and practice of the Jewish people in the beginning of the Christian period is not throughout to be measured after that in the Midrash and Talmud. For in the Midrash and Talmud the foolish reference of the psalm to Abraham predominates. Single rays of light indeed appear, as when it is said that the rod of Jacob, the rod of Judah, the rod of Moses,

IMAGE OF MESSIAH SEPARATED FROM DAVID.

mentation of the Lord (Mark xii. 35–37 and parallels) stands or falls as untrue, or only indirectly true.

The prophecy also raises itself in this psalm upon a typical foundation; for David also had his throne upon Zion beside Yahweh, but only so far as the ark of the covenant was the sacramental sign of the presence of the supramundane One. Even David emulated the priests in his care for the sanctuary of Yahweh and its endowment, but without himself being a priest or being called one, only as *episcopus circa sacra*; and the combat against the enemies of Yahweh and of the one sitting at His right hand clothes itself in words and images which remind us of the Ammonitish-Syrian war which ended with the conquest of Rabbah. But the two divine utterances, one of which significantly begins with נאם ה׳, and the other, introduced as most solemnly confirmed by Yahweh, prove that here we have to do, not only with the expression of the type which the Spirit had elevated to predictive words, but with direct immediate prophecy. This may

---

the rod of Aaron, the rod of the king, are all united in the rod which will be given to the Messiah, in order that He may conquer the peoples of the world. But the reference to Abraham ever recurs and is amalgamated with the reference to the Messiah, since it is said, the holy, blessed be His name, will command the Messiah to sit at His right hand and Abraham at His left. Obadiah Sforno comes nearer the truth, for he places the angel of service, instead of Abraham, on the left side, and gives the entire psalm a Messianic explanation; but the most celebrated interpreters, as Rashi, Aben Ezra, and Kimchi, are not willing to know anything about a Messianic interpretation. Obadiah Sforno, the Cabbalistic interpreter, stands alone.

be disputed, but it remains ever fixed, that the one addressed is a Davidic king placed in the light of the Messianic ideal, and that the psalm must acquire for the congregation, as part of their hymn and prayer book, an eschatological Messianic meaning, and that only so in the mouth of the pre-Christian congregation could it have any reasonable sense. The reciprocal relation in which Zech. vi. 12 f. stands to it proves that it is to be understood thus, and not otherwise. The one addressed appears first as ruler at the right hand of God; his people, who most willingly crowd around him, in order with him to fight for him, resemble in numbers and freshness and origin the dew born from the womb of the dawn of the morning; and without speaking of military armament, it is said that he is clothed with holy, that is, with beautiful garments of divine service (הַדְרֵי, unfolding, from הַדְרַת, 2 Chron. xx. 21 f.[1]),—it is a priestly people, and (thus the transition from ver. 3 is mediated to ver. 4) its leader is priest and king in one person, to whom Yahweh has sworn an everlasting priesthood, which is united with the kingdom after the order of Melchizedek. Nevertheless this transfiguration of the royal image does not win its way; the ruler who with God's help acquires power through bloody war predominates. We see in this a sign, which is not the only one, that the psalm, and not the prophecy of Zechariah, is the older

---

[1] The reading בהדרי is protected through ἐν ταῖς λαμπρότησι of the Septuagint against the reading בהררי, and מִשְׁחַר is unassailable; it is related to שַׁחַר, as מחשך, Isa. xlii. 16, to הֹשֶׁךְ.

IMAGE OF MESSIAH SEPARATED FROM DAVID. 93

production. Moreover, the warlike utterances in vers. 5, 6 have their parallels in the New Testament prophecy concerning the parousia of Christ in judicial glory. The colouring in Rev. xix. 11 ff. of that which Paul says in 2 Thess. ii. 8 does not sound less warlike. It is the unanimous representation of the New as well as of the Old Testament, that the kingdom of God in His Christ will ultimately make its way through fearful judgments; and the Old Testament barrier of the psalm does not consist in warlike images, since these admit of a worthy apprehension of God and of His Christ, but in this, that what the coregent of Yahweh performs as priest and that which distinguishes His people in holy adornment from other people in worldly weapons, remains veiled in silence. If we compare ver. 7, where exaltation of the head is promised to the king as a reward for his work of victory, which he follows unceasingly, with Heb. xii. 2, the deep knowledge of the historical fulfilment is remarkable. But the psalm has an essential part in the course of development toward this New Testament goal. The passage, Ps. cx. 1, is the fundamental text for the expression which so often occurs in the New Testament $\kappa\alpha\theta\iota\zeta\epsilon\iota\nu$ $\dot{\epsilon}\kappa$ $\delta\epsilon\xi\iota\hat{\omega}\nu$ $\tau o\hat{v}$ $\Theta\epsilon o\hat{v}$ as an indication of the *status exaltationis*. No psalm finds in the New Testament an echo voiced so many times as this.[1] Even $\delta\iota\acute{o}$, Phil. ii. 9, is an echo of עַל־כֵּן in ver. 7b,

---

[1] But it deserves to be remarked that the thoroughly mistaken translation of מרחם ורנו by the Septuagint ἐκ γαστρὸς πρὸ ἑωσφόρου ἐγέννησά σε is disregarded by the New Testament writers.

although that which the Psalmist says, in comparison with the utterance of the apostle, is simply a prismatic ray of the future.

§ 19. *David's Testamentary Words.*

After the promise of Nathan (2 Sam. vii.) it is established that the Messiah is to be a Son (a descendant) of David. David is the theocratic king, and the Messiah is the realized ideal of the theocratic king. We should be compelled to conclude, without express testimonies from David's moral and religious experience as accredited by history, that David more and more recognised how unlike this ideal he was. But aside from Ps. cx. we have another express testimony for this in his "last words," 2 Sam. xxiii. 1–7 ; this epilogue of his life, which is joined on to Ps. xviii., according to the standpoint of an inward relationship. As in the 110th Psalm, so these testamentary words indicate their prophetic character even in their beginning, which remind us of the utterances of Balaam (Num. xxiv. 3 f., 15 f.). Upon his dying bed David must be more strongly conscious than ever of the difference between his life and the ideal of the divinely-anointed One. Once more all the glory with which God had graciously blessed him comes before his soul. He feels that he is "the man who was raised up on high, the anointed of the God of Jacob, the singer of the lovely songs of Israel," and as an instrument of the inspiring Spirit of God : but he has been this, and now he is to die; he who, in Ps. xvi., felt himself raised above death and Hades, is brought as a languishing old man to taste of death. At this point he turns from his present condition, embraces the promise, and looks as a prophet into the future of his seed: "The God of Israel hath spoken, the Rock of Israel hath discoursed unto me: a ruler of men, a righteous, a ruler in the fear of God, and as the light of the dawn, when the sun rises, a cloudless morning, when from sunshine, from rain, green springs out of the earth."[1] This image of the future (vers. 3*b*, 4), introduced as a promise of God which cannot be broken, is nothing else than the image of the Messiah, which has been entirely released from the subjectivity of David, and placed before him. "For" —as in ver. 5 he adds, by way of explanation, the distinction which lies in this promise—"not merely so [small] is my house with God,[2] but He hath estab-

---

[1] The explanation: "If one rules over men in the fear of God, he is like," etc.,—so that what is said is set before David as a model, as Rashi and others maintain, has this, so far as the syntax is concerned, against it, that ver. 4, which begins with וכאור, does not appear as the apodosis of a conditional sentence. Everything from 3*b*–4 is a complex subject, an image placed by God before the eyes of David, to which a future—such an one will arise, and he will be, etc.—is to be supplied. The Targum divides the designations in ver. 3*b* between God and the Future One in a remarkable way: "He who rules over the children of men as a righteous judge has said (promised) to set me a King Messiah, who will finally arise and rule in the fear of the Lord."

[2] We understand לֹא־כֵן according to Job ix. 35, Num. xiii. 33, Isa. li. 6, as spoken with a gesture of disdain, "not (merely) so."

lished an everlasting covenant for me, ordered in all ways, and well assured; for all my salvation, and all that is desired[1] (by me), should He not cause it to spring?"[2] Although he dies, nevertheless the ideal of the Messiah will be realized within his house. His sun sets in order to rise all the more gloriously. While the enemies of the kingdom of promise shall be burned up as abominable thorns,[3] the salvation promised David will spring up, since it shall have a

---

[1] וְכָל־חֵפֶץ is to be understood after the model of Ex. xv. 2 (וזמרת=וזמרתי), as equivalent to וכל־חפצי, and also is to be understood according to 1 Kings v. 23, 24, as equivalent to וכל־חפצו, not as equivalent to וכל־חפצי, according to Isa. xlviii. 14, cf. liii. 10. The Targum has the right rendering: וְכָל־בָּעוּתִי.

[2] Since כי לא cannot be established in the sense of *annon* (should he not?), כי is to be considered the emphatic repetition of the preceding כי and לא (as a question with an interrogative accent without an interrogative word), equivalent to הלא; cf. כי הלא, 2 Sam. xix. 23. Wellhausen, since he reads חפצי הלא, removes the difficult כי.

[3] The adjective מֻנָד (Septuagint ἐξωσμένη) gives only in the sense of driven away, equivalent to abominated, a sense which fits the connection. A conjectural נמאס lies too far away, rather (כקוץ) מדבר, according to Judg. viii. 7, 16. The meaningless בַּשֶּׁבֶת has been erroneously introduced from ver. 7 into ver. 8 (Wellhausen); for it cannot signify "on the spot" (Keil and Kimchi), and in this sense it would be without significance [for the passage]. We might rather translate with annihilation, with peremptory judgment (Jerome, *usque ad nihilum*); but שֶׁבֶת forms neither in Biblical nor in post-Biblical Hebrew a derivative שֶׁבֶת. Hence [we are to understand] that they [the thorns] are not seized with the hand, but that they are seized by one armed with a long-handled spear, in order to take hold of them and to cast them into the fire.

bodily reality in a scion of his house. This word יַצְמִיחַ [he shall cause to sprout] becomes later a favourite expression of Messianic prophecy (Jer. xxxiii. 15; Ezek. xxix. 21; Ps. cxxxii. 17); and צֶמַח [sprout], after the way has been prepared through Isa. iv. 2 and Jer. xxiii. 5, xxxiii. 15, becomes fully the name of the Messiah in Zechariah.

§ 20. *Messianic Desires and Hopes of Solomon.*

But the time when the Messiah as an eschatological person is contrasted with the untheocratic Davidic kingdom of the present is still far away. The testamentary words of David do not justify the supposition that he represents the realization of the Messianic promise as belonging to the extreme end of a line of rulers arising from him. We need not be surprised, therefore, when Solomon in the seventy-second Psalm, which bears in all its peculiar lineaments the stamp of a Solomonic origin, makes the Messianic image which God had placed before the soul of his dying father, since it contains nothing superhuman, as a precious legacy, his ideal; and that, entering on his reign, he cherished the wish that in his person the Messianic idea, and through his government the Messianic age, might be realized, whether it be that he utters the wish for himself, or puts it in the mouth of the people as a petition and hope.

The psalm begins (ver. 1) with a petition made directly to God, which passes over (vers. 2–8) into the form of a wish; the wishes then become hopes (vers. 9–15), and these again, in ver. 16 f., wishes. The expression of the thoughts therefore is predominatingly optative. The wish (ver. 6): "May He come down like rain upon meadow grass, as powerful showers upon the earth,"[1] reminds us of 2 Sam. xxiii. 4, where the effect of the parousia of the Messiah is compared with the greenness of the earth after a fertilizing warm rain. The wish: "May He rule from sea to sea, and from the river to the ends of the earth," sounds like an echo from Num. xxiv. 19 in Balaam's prophecy. And the wish, 17b, "May they bless themselves in Him, may all nations call Him blessed," applies the old promise concerning the blessing of the peoples in the seed of the patriarchs to the Messiah of Israel. All the peoples of the world may wish themselves the blessing of the divinely-chosen and blessed one, hence wonderingly and desirous of salvation they may subject themselves to Him. The psalm is not directly, but only indirectly prophetic, since it is wished that in Solomon may be fulfilled what is predicted and hoped of the Messiah. These wishes have all to a certain extent been fulfilled in Solomon, yet so that the Messianic ideal over against the glory of Solomon preserved its transcendent character, in order that it might

---

[1] We do not change זַרְזִיף, with Cheyne, into יַרְדִיף. Precisely this accumulation of synonyms appears to us to be a characteristic of the style of Solomon, as it is a characteristic element of the introductory Proverbs (chaps. i.–ix., see v. 14, 19, cf. v. 11, vi. 7, vii. 9, viii. 13, 31).

be evident that its proper fulfilment lay in the domain of the future.

§ 21. *Prophecy and Chokma.*

The seventy-second Psalm is not directly a prophetic psalm, nor is a Psalm directly prophetic to be expected from Solomon. While it is related concerning David, that with his anointing through Samuel the Spirit of Yahweh came over him (1 Sam. xvi. 13), the anointing of Solomon by Zadok appears to be more of a worldly than of a spiritual circumstance (1 Kings i. 39). David received in Bethlehem, with the anointing, the spirit of prophecy, which raised him above the bounds of his nature, and initiated him into the secrets of the works and ways of the God of Israel. But Solomon entreated for himself in Gibeon the insight which was necessary for him as ruler and judge, and received the promise of a wise and understanding heart without a parallel (1 Kings iii. 12). His peculiar gift was wisdom which looked through the things of this world, and made itself serviceable, and knew how to ennoble it through a moral religious apprehension.

As Solomon, according to his name, was the man of peace (אִישׁ מְנוּחָה, 1 Chron. xxii. 9), that is, of a luxurious peace, which he enjoyed, which blossomed from the struggles and distresses of the Davidic age, there culminated in general with him the wide-hearted, more cosmopolitan than national tendency of his age, which entered into competition with the peoples in artificial products of the mind, as well as in commercial undertakings and buildings. The intellectual life took on under him the character of the gnosis, which sought to establish the contents of the pistis in a speculative way. The time of the Chokma began, which is turned less to revelation on the side of the history of redemption than to it on the side of a common humanity, and it sought to lay hold of the universal ideas on which even then the predisposition of a Yahweh religion to a world religion was recognisable.

The time of Solomon became the time of the efflorescence of the Chokma literature. For the foundation of the Book of Proverbs, which moves in the checkered variety of the circumstances of human life, and is divided into rules of life rooted in the fear of God, is Solomonic.

The Song of Songs, which celebrates the relation of that sacred love which is common to men, is not wanting in internal evidence of Solomon's authorship.

And for the origin of the Book of Job there is no time better fitted than the age of Solomon and its Chokma associations, out of which has gone forth the original book as well as the section of Elihu, which seeks to bring back his boldness to the proper degree of moderation. The Book of Job, so to speak, is a poem of religious philosophy, which in the form of a dramatized history of a righteous man, outside of Israel, seeks to answer the question concerning the divine motive and object in the sufferings of a righteous man, and, rightly understood, answers it for all time from the standpoint of divine love, and in the participation of those who love God, and who are loved by Him in securing the ends of the world's history. We emphasize three passages of this wonderful book (xvii. 3, xix. 23–27, xxxiii. 23 f.), which show that the Chokma on its side, as well as prophecy, prepares the way for the parousia of the God-man, and the transition of the religion of Israel into Christianity.

Remark.—If the Song of Songs were an allegorical poem, it would be a prophetical production. The Targum paraphrases it as a picture of the history of Israel from the exodus out of Egypt, reaching into the Messianic period. For this reason it is a constituent part of the liturgy of the eighth Passover day. Shulamith is regarded as an image of Israel, and Solomon as an image of God. All שלמה of the Song of Songs—according to an ancient saying—are holy, excepting viii. 11, namely, as a figurative indication (כנוי) of the God of peace. Naturally the traditional churchly explanation understood the Solomon of the Song of Songs as an image of Christ, that is, of the Messiah who appeared in Jesus. But the allegorical interpretation shows that it cannot be carried through. The figurative interpretation of all details falls into a boundless arbitrariness, and loses itself in scandalous absurdities. Solomon was not a prophet of the future Messiah, and still less did he make his own person in an allegorical way the image of the Messiah. But he was a type of Christ, and Shulamith of Galilee, Solomon's companion picture, can be considered as a type of the Church, raised by Christ out of a lowly condition to a fellowship with him in love and glory. In the Syrian Bible the Song of Songs is called *chekmat chekmátá*, that is, wisdom of wisdom (*Weisheit der Weisheiten*). It is a Chokma book, which, as a part of the canon, is a riddle challenging acumen. As a Chokma book it has so far its place, as it has not a contents which is national, but common to all mankind, and in a pious, clever way celebrates pure, true sexual love; but it has become a part of the canon only, as we may assume, because its prophetic sense is presupposed. It is, however, not direct prophecy, but a typical shadow which is first rightly to be understood from the standpoint of the history of fulfilment of the loving relation, not of God, but of the God-man to His Church.

§ 22. *The Goël and the Mediating Angel in the Book of Job.*

It is one-sided and misleading when we seek the preparation for the New Testament in the Old solely in genuine Messianic prophecy. The progressive knowledge of God the Redeemer is just as important a side of the preparation as the progressive knowledge of the world-wide rule of the second David. This latter, as we shall see farther on, must be satisfied in the Old Testament with a radical transformation, in order to blend with the knowledge of God the Redeemer in a way corresponding to the divine decree which is consummated in the New Testament. The Book of Job has an important part in furthering the knowledge of salvation on the divine side. The

GOËL AND ANGELUS INTERNUNTIUS IN JOB. 103

friends of Job consider his great sufferings as the punishment of great sins, and in this way heighten his inward trial, for he is conscious of his previous state of grace, although he appears to be a target of the divine wrath, without knowing in what way he has brought it upon him. The wise love, according to which God acts, is turned into sovereign caprice. But gradually the clouds are broken, and the knowledge that this God cannot be absolutely arbitrary begins to dawn upon him.

In xvii. 3 he prays to God that God might deposit a pledge (שִׂימָה נָּא), and give security (עָרְבֵנִי) to Himself (עִמָּךְ), the God of love to the God of wrath. It is the fundamental idea of the New Testament Gospel concerning the reconciliation (καταλλαγή) which flashes forth here. God is conceived of as two kinds of persons: as Judge, who treats Job as worthy of punishment; and as Surety, who pledges Himself before the Judge for the innocence of the sufferer, and at the same time gives bail. And in xix. 23–27 he presses through to the postulate of faith, that even if his skin should be completely [1] destroyed, and his outer man should be dissolved in the dust of the grave, yet the truth would break through the false appearance, and wrath would give place to love, and God the

---

[1] The signification of "completely" is involved in אחר, and זאת signifies adverbially, "in this manner." The connection forbids that we should take it together with עוֹרִי, according to הדור זו, Ps. xii. 8. The subject of נִקְּפוּ are the hidden powers of destruction.

living one, outlasting everything, would appear for him the dead, and coming forth out of His hiding-place, would permit him with the eyes of the other world to behold Him as his גֹּאֵל, that is, as the avenger of his blood which is regarded as that of a criminal, as a ransomer of his honour which has fallen into disgrace, as a redeemer from the curse which rested upon him, above all things, from the consciousness of divine wrath, whose decree seemed to have occasioned his sufferings. As that which he begs in xvii. 3 appears in 2 Cor. v. 19 as performed through God in Christ for the whole world; so Rom. viii. 34 shows into what a confession of firm confidence Job's וַאֲנִי יָדַעְתִּי גֹּאֲלִי חָי is transformed from the New Testament standpoint. The human side of this divine work of redemption is not considered in these bold words of faith. But in the section of Elihu we see the preparation for a recognition of a Mediator between God and man, since from the elevation of man out of the depth of the guilt of sin, and the condition of punishment, the following representation is presented in xxxiii. 23, 24: "If with him [the sinner who stands on the brink of death and hell] an angel is present[1] as mediator (מלאך מליץ), one of a thousand (that is, pre-eminent above a thousand) to announce to man what is for his advantage. He (God) has compassion on him, and says: Let him go free, that he may not go down into the grave—I have demanded an

[1] We understand עָלָיו as in נִצָּב עָלָיו, to stand by any one, Gen. xviii. 2, xlv. 1, and elsewhere.

expiatory payment" (כֹּפֶר, a λύτρον covering sin and guilt). Here we see in the Book of Job, which is elsewhere remarkable for its angelology, that the redemption of man can only be mediated by means of a superhuman being. The *angelus internuntius* is a preformation of the Redeemer going forth from the range of the Godhead. The angelic form is the oldest, which the hope of a mediator of salvation gives (Gen. xlviii. 16).[1] It is taken up again—to remark even here by way of anticipation—in Mal. iii. 1 (cf. also the remarkable translation of the Septuagint of Isa. ix. 5). The מלאך הברית of prophecy is the reality of the מלאך מליץ postulated by the Chokma.

[1] Cf. on this passage, Kemmler, *Hiob oder Kamp und Sieg im Leiden*, Stuttgart 1876; and Rogge, *Das Buch Hiob, der Gemeinde dargeboten*, Erlangen 1877.

CHAPTER VI.

PROPHECY AND CHOKMA IN THE FIRST EPOCHS OF THE DIVISION OF THE KINGDOM.

§ 23. *The Prophets after the Division of the Kingdom until the Reign of Jehoshaphat and the Dynasty of Omri.*

NATHAN bound the Messianic promise for ever to the house of David, and Gad, since he directed David to erect an altar upon the threshing-floor of Araunah (Chronicler, Ornan) the Jebusite, laid the foundation for the temple upon Moriah (2 Chron. iii. 1), in which Israel, praying and sacrificing for over a thousand years, honoured God. But we have no prophetic writings or public addresses, handed down by tradition, of either of these two prophets, or of the prophets of the first six or seven decades after the division of the kingdom, of whom Ahijah, Jedi (Iddo), Jehu ben Chanani appeared in the kingdom of Israel, and Shemaiah, Iddo, Azariah ben Oded, Chanani in the kingdom of Judah. The Books of Kings and Chronicles make us acquainted with the interference of these prophets in the history of the times, and with the words which accompanied their deeds. Their attitude to the Messianic hope is withdrawn from our knowledge. But granted that their utterances, although freely reproduced, are still not without connection with tradition, these prophets appear in many thoughts and forms of thought connected with the Messianic hope as forerunners of the later prophets.

The prophetic word of Obadiah (ver. 17) and Joel (iii. 5) concerning a פְּלֵיטָה [an escaping] of Israel, which is to participate in salvation, after judgment has gone forth, was uttered even by Shemaiah under Jeroboam (2 Chron. xii. 7); and in the prophecy of Hosea concerning Israel's final repentance and conversion (iii. 4 f., v. 15) we seem to have the echo of the prophecy of Azariah under Asa (2 Chron. xv. 31), as well as of the word of Ahijah the Shilonite, that a lamp (נִיר=נֵר) shall remain for David (1 Kings xi. 36), which is a favourite expression for a promise given to David (1 Kings xv. 4; 2 Kings viii. 19; 2 Chron. xxi. 7; Ps. cxxxii. 17).

But we do not perceive anything at all which can be placed in connection with the Messianic hope in that which the historical books relate concerning the prophets of the following royal historical epoch, from Jehoshaphat and Ahab to Amaziah and Jeroboam II., namely, the Chronicles, concerning Jehu ben Chanani, Jahaziel ben Zechariah, Eliezer ben Dodawahu, and the martyr Zechariah ben Jehoida; and the Book of Kings, concerning Micaiah ben Imlah (see his address, 1 Kings xxii. 17–23), and concerning the two gigantic, wonderful prophets Elijah and Elisha.

108 MESSIANIC PROPHECIES IN HISTORICAL SUCCESSION.

In all which these prophets do and say there is no occasion for a testimony of Messianic significance, not even in the words which accompany Elijah's and Elisha's deeds. Their calling is directed to contend against heathenism, and in distinction from the prophets of the worship of Baal and Astarte, and of Yahweh under the form of a steer, to train up prophets of the one supernatural holy God. But it would be a wrong conclusion from silence if we should deny the Messianic hope to all these. None of the prophets of Judah or Israel denounces the division of the kingdom. All recognise that it stands *de jure*. But true religiousness would not be possible in Israel as in Judah unless there were connected with it the longing for the removal of the divine decree, and therefore for a king over the reunited kingdom, for another David, for the Messiah.

§ 24. *The Metaphysical Conception of Wisdom in the Introduction to the Book of Proverbs.*

While the Messianic proclamation of the prophets appears to have run dry, the extra-national pure religious enrichment and deepening of the knowledge of salvation is continued. The Book of Proverbs, which belongs to this literature, has for its chief parts two collections of Solomonic proverbs, of which the younger, as is indicated in xxv. 1, was revised by the "Men of Hezekiah." There is no more favourable time for editing the older collection than the period of

Jehoshaphat, the king who, more perhaps than any other, seemed to be concerned for the promotion of the training of the people upon the ground of true religiousness (2 Chron. xvii. 7–9).

There follow upon the title and motto of the older collection of proverbs (i. 1–7) in i. 8–ix., connected addresses in the form of proverbs, which serve the מִשְׁלֵי שְׁלֹמֹה (the Proverbs of Solomon x. 1) as an introduction, and, directing themselves especially to the youth, commend the wisdom which is rooted in the fear of God. The one who utters the prologue speaks here as a father to his children, but three times he introduces Wisdom herself as speaking (i. 20 ff., viii. 1 ff., ix. 1–12). He calls her חָכְמָה or חָכְמוֹת (i. 20, ix. 1), which is just such an intensive plural as אֱלֹהִים. She comes forth publicly after the manner of a street preacher and travelling teacher. She appears as a person of divine character, for she promises (i. 23) those who return to her a participation in her spirit, and it is presupposed (ver. 28) that prayer is offered to her, and that she causes prayers to be answered, or even unanswered. The personification, in itself considered, can be regarded just as purely allegorical as that of folly (ix. 13). But the question ever recurs, What is the conception which the author has of this Wisdom who gives forth the spirit from herself, and is to be called upon in prayer? It appears from her testimony that, in his opinion, she is more than a personified characteristic, more than a personified good (viii. 22–31): " Yahweh hath brought me forth [1] as the firstling of His way [of His activity, which had its end in a world of creatures], before any of His works from the beginning. From everlasting I was established, from the very first, from the primitive commencement of the earth. When the depths of water did not exist, I was born, when the fountains did not exist, laden with water. Before the mountains were settled, before the hills I was born—when He had not yet worked out the earth and the fields, and the sum of the particles of dust of the earth. When He prepared the heaven I was there, when He measured off a circle about the surface of the depths of water. When He fastened the heights of ether above, when the sources of the depths of the waters broke forth mightily, when He set to the sea its bounds, that the waters should not transgress His commands; when He measured off the foundations of the earth, then I was by him as a workman,[2] and I carried on a joyous play daily, gamboling before Him all the time, gamboling in the world of His earth, and carrying on my joyous play among the children of men."

Five thoughts come in this self-testimony of Wisdom

[1] The Targum and the Syriac version translate בְּרָאַנִי, which is inadmissible; for, in the view of the author, the bringing forth of Wisdom preceded בראשית ברא (מעשה בראשית), she is therefore not even a work of creation.

[2] The noun אמון forms no feminine, and has therefore, like *artifex*, two genders. It is here considered as feminine; but, since Wisdom is to be thought of as without gender, is not to be translated as a feminine δημιουργός (cf. nevertheless Wisd. vii. 21, τεχνῖτις).

to pictorial expression: (1) she was born of God before the creation of the world; (2) she was present as this came into being; (3) she took on by it a mediating position, since God in the execution of His thoughts of creation made use of her mediation; (4) this service which she rendered to God, the Creator, was for her a delightful pleasure; (5) the dearest circle of her activity, but within the entire creation, was the earth and the men upon it.

As the Spirit of God is a power which goes forth from God, which makes alive that which is to be created, and maintains in life that which is created; so Wisdom is a power born of God, which makes that a reality which is to be created in the manner willed by God, and which helps free creatures, especially men, to the attainment of the end divinely willed. If we thought of these powers, ejected from God, as special divine existences separated from God, we should have a mythological representation which could not be harmonized with the unity of God. The true state of the case should rather be represented, that God, as the origin of being, discloses the Spirit and the Wisdom from Himself as special ways of the manifestation of His being. Spirit and Wisdom are powers originating in the being of the one God, and surrounded by His one being. Without finding in it the trinitarian dogma, we nevertheless ascertain that the Old Testament Scriptures, since on their first page they discriminate between אֱלֹהִים and רוּחַ אֱלֹהִים, do not conceive of God as an inflexible *monas*, and that, since the חָכְמָה enters as *causa media* of God's relation to the world, the one being of God is represented as threefold. As in the Old Testament history the way is prepared for the New Testament revelation of God, since it distinguishes between God and His Spirit and His Angel, in which His name, that is, the self-revelation of His being, is to be made; so the way is prepared in the Old Testament Chokma literature, since it distinguishes between God and His Spirit and His Wisdom. It is remarkable that the utterances of Wisdom in Prov. i. and viii. correspond remarkably with the utterances of Jesus in the Gospel of John. Even the beginning of John i. 1, ἐν ἀρχῇ ἦν ὁ λόγος, is related in contents to the ה' קָנָנִי רֵאשִׁית דַּרְכּוֹ (Prov. viii. 22). And when the apostle (Col. i. 16) says of Christ: τὰ πάντα δι' αὐτοῦ καὶ εἰς αὐτὸν ἔκτισται, this can be transformed, according to Prov. viii. 22–31, into the utterance that Wisdom, which was the mediatrix of the creation of the world, and is the ideal goal of the world's history, has appeared in Him historically and bodily.

§ 25. *The Epithalamium, Ps.* xlv.

Our view is now again turned from the moralizing and dogmatizing Chokma to lyric poetry, which moves in hopes and wishes; for, as we go farther from the period of Jehoshaphat's reign, the forty-fifth Psalm draws our attention to itself, which we hold, for probable reasons which we have expressed elsewhere,—cf. ver. 9 with 1 Kings xxii. 39; Amos iii. 15,—for an epithalamium composed on the marriage of Joram, the son of Jehoshaphat, with Athaliah, the daughter of the wife of Ahab, sprung from the royal house of Tyre. Without holding our view as infallible, we consider that it is sufficiently established, so that we are subjectively justified in attributing this psalm to the time of Jehoshaphat and Joram. But whether the king whom the poet celebrates was Joram, or perhaps some one else, it remains permanently established (1) that he stands before the poet in the light of Messianic exaltation and destiny, and (2) that he did not justify the wedding wishes and expectations. In three places the one who is celebrated is raised beyond the bounds of time into the sphere of the unending. "Thou art endowed with beauty," says ver. 3, "more than the children of men. Grace is poured out upon thy lips, therefore Elohim hath blessed thee for ever" (לְעוֹלָם). The beauty and the grace of his appearance make the impression of an imperishable blessing. And the conclusion of ver. 18 is: "I will extol thy name in all generations, therefore peoples will praise thee for ever and ever" (לְעֹלָם וָעֶד), — the poet, speaking in the name of the immortal congregation, knows beforehand that his praise of this king will be spread abroad in ever wider circles over the entire inhabited world, and will resound for ever. In ver. 7 he even appears to address אֱלֹהִים: "Thy throne, Elohim, endures for ever and ever" (עוֹלָם וָעֶד). The Epistle to the Hebrews (i. 8 f.), at least, proceeds from the understanding of this אֱלֹהִים as a vocative, and we may correct or explain as we will, ver. 7a is certainly not an address to God. The three utterances, whether Solomon or Joram, or whoever else may be this king, are hyperboles, but which have nothing in common with the royal apotheoses of courtly Oriental poetry. The poet cherishes really the transcendent hope that the young king who is about to be married will realize the ideal of the theocratic kingdom, and hence the Messianic idea. The one celebrated nevertheless disappointed these high expectations, and far from being an object of universal and everlasting praise, he has disappeared. But, on the other hand, the poet was in so far not deceived, since he really, as two thousand years ago, yet sings the praise of the divine King in this song which still exists. For since this psalm was received into the hymn-book of the Church, it has ceased to be a song written for a special occasion. It is, according to the prophetic word, to be understood as a song of praise to King Messiah, and for the New Testament Church, for which, more than for the Old Testament, all sensuous elements have been transformed into supersensuous, it is a song of the "marriage of the Lamb," closely related to the Song of Songs as mystically understood.

Remark.—As Canticles, antitypically and hence mystically understood, remains out of the range of the Old Testament progress of the knowledge of salvation, and could only be taken into account when, in the view of the poet himself, it was an allegorical picture; so Ps. xlv., first through the signification which the congrega-

THE EPITHALAMIUM. 115

tion connects with it, which Hermann Schultz in his *Old Testament Theology* calls "the second meaning of Scripture," becomes eschatological and Messianic. The praise of the poet himself is connected with a king who belongs to his own time, whom he regards as fulfilling the Messianic hope, in so far as he appears to him in his heavenly beauty, his irresistible power, his moral purity and elevation, the full realization of the close relation in which David and his seed is placed to God. But this king marries a king's daughter, and his throne is eternal only through inheritance (בָּנֶיךָ, 17*a*). These are characteristics which do not enrich the image of the Messiah, but only cloud it; for the Messiah, as is predicated in the Old Testament, is raised above the earthly conditions of marriage and of the blessing of children. His throne is eternal, because it has eternal duration in Him, and without being inherited outside of Himself. These characteristics, which are occasioned by the origin of the song as a marriage poem, demand for the psalm as a church, and at the same time as a New Testament hymn, a spiritual metamorphosis. And in view of these characteristics, the interpretation of אֱלֹהִים, 17*a*, as a vocative is improbable, and, presupposing the primitive character of the text, is to be translated, "Thy throne of Elohim (cf. the syntax of 2 Sam. xxii. 33) is for ever and ever," that is, the throne which thou takest as anointed of God. The author of the Epistle to the Hebrews cites and uses the passage according to the Greek text.

CHAPTER VII.

THE MESSIANIC ELEMENTS IN THE PROPHETIC LITERATURE FROM JORAM TO HEZEKIAH.

§ 26. *The Relation of the three oldest Prophetic Writings to the Messianic Idea.*

THE greatest oratorical development of the power of prophecy falls in the period of the world empires, which is opened by the conflict of Israel (Ephraim), and then of Judah with Assyria, which was brought on by the attack on Judah through the allied kingdoms of Syria and Ephraim. This Syro-Ephraimitic war arose in the last years of Jotham. The year of the death of his father Uzziah,—according to the Biblical records, 755 B.C.,—in which Isaiah was called, is the boundary of the splendid period of prophetic literature and of its forerunners Obadiah, Joel, and Amos. Obadiah prophesies under Joram the son and successor of Jehoshaphat, after the apostasy of Edom from the Davidic supremacy (2 Kings viii. 22; 2 Chron. xxi. 10), the punishment which is to come upon Edom; Joel had that apostasy, with which the slaughter of the Judaeans dwelling in Idumea was connected (iii. 19 ff.), still in fresh remembrance; and his book mirrors a time of the well-arranged service of Yahweh as it existed in the first half of the government of Joash (about 850 B.C.), but no longer in the second. Amos' appearance occurs, according to the superscription of his book, in the time of Uzziah, two years before the earthquake, and as the contents of the book shows, in the time of the last century of Jeroboam II., the first of Uzziah,—the round of judgments announced by him begins with Damascus (cf. i. 4 with 2 Kings viii. 12, xiii. 22), and falls then, as in Joel on Philistia, which was still tributary under Jehoshaphat (2 Chron. xvii. 11), on Phoenicia and Edom. But these prophets are still more closely entwined together through their mutual relationship to the misfortune under Joram (2 Chron. xxi. 16 f., xxii. 1); the attack upon Judah through hordes of Philistines and Arabs, the slaying of all the children of Joram except Ahaziah, and the carrying away of a great part of the Judaeans, and especially of the inhabitants of Jerusalem, which were sold partly to the Phoenicians, and partly by these and the Edomites to the Greeks of Asia Minor (Obad. ver. 20; Joel iii. 1–8; Amos i. 6–10), afford a picture, in which the elements are mutually supplementary, of this prelude of the following great exile.

But in order to secure a right picture of the relations of the most ancient literary prophets—that is, of those whose writings we possess—to the Messianic idea, and not a picture which is distorted through a misleading argumentation *e silentio*, we must take Obadiah, Joel, and Amos together. In Obadiah it is מוֹשִׁעִים, victorious deliverers, who march from the mountain of Zion to the mountain of Esau in order to punish a malicious hereditary enemy (21*a*); but in Joel it is Yahweh, who dwells in Zion, who does not suffer the brother's blood shed by Edom to go unavenged (iv. 21); and in Amos, who has survived the deep humiliation of Judah and its king through the proud more powerful northern kingdom, and the worst in the demolition of the walls of Jerusalem through Joash, the father and predecessor of Jeroboam II. (2 Kings xiv. 13), it is the house of David restored, through which Edom is again subjugated (Amos ix. 11 f.): " On that day I will raise up the hut of David which is fallen, and wall up its breaches [of the walls]; and that which is torn down [of David] I will build up as in the days of old, in order that they may take possession of the remnant of Edom, and of all the peoples upon whom my name has been named [1] [as belonging to the kingdom of my anointed]." This is not an immediate Messianic prophecy, but the raising up again of the house of David is of like import with the promise of another David, an antitype of David and Solomon. If the prophecy were taken more personally, nevertheless it would not for this reason have a more New Testament character,

[1] Instead of לְמַעַן יִירְשׁוּ אֶת שְׁאֵרִית אֱדוֹם, the Septuagint reads למען ידרשו שארית אדם ($ὅπως ἐκζητήσωσιν οἱ κατάλοιποι τῶν ἀνθρώπων$), without an object. The [reading] $τὸν κύριον$, which is added in the Alexandrian MS., probably was taken from Rev. xv. 17. We see from the previous use of the passage that the Septuagint was esteemed almost as highly as the primitive text.

for the fundamental character of the image of the Messiah at [this] time is still a righteous dominion establishing peace, which rises upon the foundation of victorious primitive wars, and because it is exercised in the name of the one true, holy God it also makes an overpowering impression upon the world outside of Israel. It is therefore an anachronism, which offends against the development of the Messianic proclamation, when some, as Luther, following Jerome, understand by מוֹרֶה לִצְדָקָה, promised in Joel ii. 23, the Messiah as instructor in righteousness. If the words were to be translated thus, the prophet must mean himself under this divinely-given teacher, who instructed the people in the conduct which was in accordance with salvation (לְ like אֶל, 2 Chron. vi. 27), through which it can be free from the destinies under which it now suffers. We have not here to examine whether it is not rather intended: "According to the measure [as it must where the cultivation of the land is blessed] of the beginning of the early rain," since it lies outside of the range of our investigation.

For the very reason that the knowledge given prophetically has not yet advanced so far as to connect with the ideal king of the future the representation of a teacher who proclaims the way of salvation, we do not miss the Messiah in the three prophets, but rejoice all the more in the great New Testament ideas uttered by them, which, when the true Messiah shall appear, will take an essential place in the proclamation with which He stands forth, and in the religion of the Messiah, that is, in Christianity, which has Him as its centre. The aim of the history of the world, according to the closing words of Obadiah's prophecy, is this, that Yahweh may have the royal rule (וְהָיְתָה לה' הַמְּלוּכָה), hence the realization and completion of the kingdom of God. The conception of the kingdom of God has not yet in Obadiah the fulness and depth of meaning which it secured when Jesus Christ appeared among the people with the preaching of the gospel of the kingdom of God; but when, according to Mark i. 15, He said: "The time is fulfilled, and the kingdom of God has come; repent, and believe on the gospel," He certainly means that now the time has passed which was determined according to God's decree for the transition of the prophecy which was begun by Obadiah concerning the future kingdom of God, to the gospel which now appears in reality. And while in Obadiah the breaking through of the kingdom of God is really prepared by bloody war and victory, by the extension of the dominion of the people of God, and by bringing home those of their own people who have been delivered into slavery, we hear in Joel of a pouring out of the Spirit of God upon all flesh, so that that which sounds so external in Obadiah, is spiritualized to such an extent by means of a gigantic step forward, that the apostles, in that which they experience at Pentecost after the resurrection and ascension of Jesus, see a fulfilment which corresponds with the prophecy of Joel: "And it shall come to pass afterwards," says God through the prophet, " I will pour out my spirit upon all flesh, and your sons and your daughters shall prophesy, your old men shall dream dreams, and your young men see visions. And also upon the servants and the handmaids will I pour out in those days my Spirit."

The bold image of the pouring out of the Spirit[1] has arisen since the promises pertaining to the immediate future of the pouring out of rain and of the destruction of grasshoppers are surpassed by the eschatological promises of the pouring out of the Spirit and of judgment upon the world, which is hostile to the people of God. As rain rejuvenates the natural world, so the Spirit of God works within man a new life which renders him happy, and which shows itself without as a power over the world. The pouring out of this Spirit indicates a gift in a fulness and strength which has hitherto not been experienced. Before there were individuals in Israel, especially the prophets, who stood with God through His Spirit in near confidential relations; but this spiritual life in God becomes the future possession of all, without distinction of sex and age, even of those who do not belong to the people of Israel by birth, but as servants through incorporation.

Since this expression כָּל בָּשָׂר is used especially in connection with Israel, it might appear that it does not here indicate the entire human race. But in every place where כָּל בָּשָׂר occurs it has an absolute sense. Sometimes it embraces the animals, *e.g.* Gen. vi. 13;

[1] The LXX. weakens it, since it translates אֶשְׁפּוֹךְ אֶת־רוּחִי partitively ἐκχεῶ ἀπὸ τοῦ πνεύματός μου.

but especially it indicates the whole, with reference to its material character, weakness and mortality (Isa. xl. 5; Zech. ii. 17; Ps. lxv. 3). And that Joel includes the heathen in the future salvation appears in that which he further says concerning the judgments which make way for salvation, and concerning those who are to have a part in the salvation (iii. 3-5): "And I give signs in heaven and upon earth, blood, and fire, and pillars of smoke. The sun shall be turned into darkness and the moon into blood, before the coming of the day of Yahweh, the great and terrible. And it shall come to pass that every one who shall call on the name of Yahweh shall escape: for upon Mount Zion and in Jerusalem there shall be an escaping, as Yahweh hath said, and among those who flee whom Yahweh intends to call." From here there falls upon כָּל בָּשָׂר a light which confirms the absoluteness of the conception. The divine word contained in the writing of Obadiah, בְּהַר צִיּוֹן תִּהְיֶה פְלֵיטָה, "in Mount Zion there shall be an escaping," is here repeated by Joel as a citation, in order to supplement it by another divine word which is spoken regarding it. There is to remain, not only one, but also a twofold פְלֵיטָה, "escaping," one consisting of those of the people of Israel who in the midst of judgments turn themselves to the God of salvation desiring salvation, and one consisting of the שְׂרִידִים, whom Yahweh shall call.[1] As the distinction demands,

[1] Among the old translators Jerome is the first who has correctly rendered the words וּבַשְּׂרִידִים אֲשֶׁר ה' קֹרֵא, *et in residuis*,

the mass who are to be saved out of the heathen world is intended. Those from Israel shall be saved by calling on a God who has already been revealed to them; those from the heathen by the call of mercy of the One revealing Himself to them.

While in this way the conception of כָּל בָּשָׂר, "all flesh," on the one side receives the general reference to the Israelitish people and the people outside of Israel, it is narrowed on the other, since God's people of the final period appear as the result of a judicial sifting process, which reduces the mass of Israel and of the heathen to a kernel which can withstand the fire. Amos also testifies to this sifting process (ix. 9): "For, behold I appoint and will [by means of the world power executing this appointment] shake the house of Israel, as one shakes in a sieve, and there shall not fall a grain to the earth." The chaff is blown away from the sieve which is shaken against the wind, and the rubbish and dirt falls through it; but the wheat remains in the sieve, in order to be planted in the ground of the land of promise in its time. The mass of Israel is mingled with the heathen, and perishes. The fundamental idea of Isaiah, שְׁאָר יָשׁוּב, only a remnant, but yet a remnant shall be converted, which is also a fundamental idea of the Epistle to the Romans (for, as the apostle, ix. 6, says, they are not all Israelites who are from Israel), therefore already finds expression in the three oldest prophetic writings.

quos Dominus vocaverit, according to which Luther and all the others render, "whom the Lord shall call."

It is exclusively grace which makes Israel God's people and insures its continuance. On its natural side, if the election by grace and the condition of grace is disregarded, it does not stand before God higher than the peoples of the world. Amos ix. 7: "Are ye not to me like the sons of the Cushites, children of Israel?" is Yahweh's address. "Did I not bring Israel up out of Egypt, and the Philistines from Caphtor, and Aram from Kir?" Israel, who has fallen from grace, and has sunk back into his natural condition, has nothing as an advantage above the Ethiopians, and in itself, aside from God's wonderful works, which the mass of Israel despises, and God's purposes of grace, which it renders vain, the exodus of Israel from Egypt stands on the same plane with the wanderings of the Philistines from Crete, and the Aramaeans from the neighbourhood of the river Kura.

These are New Testament thoughts in the midst of the Old Testament. Worth is not measured by God according to fleshly origin, but according to the inward relation to the God of salvation. "There is no difference," says Paul, Rom. x. 12, "between Jews and Greeks. There is one Lord of all, rich over all who call on Him: for [it is the word of Joel's, iii. 5, to which he appeals] whosoever shall call on the name of the Lord shall be saved." If we were to think away the genuine Messianic prophecy of a Christ of God from the Old Testament, Jesus would even then be the goal, fulfilment, and conclusion of the Old Testament, because through Him the New Testament ideas of the Old Testament not only have come into consciousness, but also in the history of the world have attained a decided domination.

Remark.—The Book of Jonah also deserves to be mentioned here. Even the sending of Jonah to Nineveh, in order to call to repentance through threatened judgment, is unique in the Old Testament; for in every case except this the predictions of the prophets concerning the nations proceed from the prophetic watch-tower in the land of Israel. Even Jesus considered Himself as assigned to the circle of the people of Israel. Also the apostles before the ascension of the Lord were limited to this narrow circle; and as later Peter should enter a heathen house with the preaching of salvation, he must first be freed through a heavenly vision from his opposition. Hence it is not remarkable that Jonah sought to avoid his mission to Nineveh. There is even a subjective justification for his being sullen when justice was visited upon the Ninevites instead of mercy. It was probably not common envy (as Acts xiii. 45; cf. 1 Thess. ii. 16); but he may have surmised that the reception of the heathen would result in the loss of Israel's position as children. But through the feelings which were occasioned by the *kikayon* (Ricinus), which sprang up quickly and withered as quickly, God brings him the consciousness that also the heathen, who not less than Israel have Him as their Creator and Governor, are objects of His pity. Not only through the Ninevites, but also through the heathen sailors, He shows that the heathen are in no wise given up to be lost; that also among them neither noble humaneness nor, when God the only Holy One and His will are revealed, receptivity and obedience to faith are wanting, that therefore in the heathen world there is a preparatory activity of grace which is connected with the testimony of the conscience. That which Joel testifies in chap. iii., that the heathen are embraced in the divine decree, this the Book of Jonah teaches and confirms through facts. We may date it as we will, we may explain the wonderful preservation of the prophet for his calling as we will, the remarkable anticipation of the New Testament in the Old, and the utterances of Jesus, as Matt. xii. 39—41, show how fond He was of this book, in which He found prefigured His own way leading through the grave to the heathen.

§ 27. *The View of Hosea, the Ephraimitic Prophet of the Final Period.*

Hosea, whose book is properly the Ephraimitic prophetic book, is connected with Amos the Judaean prophet, who, following the drawing of the Spirit, appeared in Bethel, the chief place of Jeroboam's worship. How long after this time his activity lasted is doubtful; but for us it is of no consequence, for those of his views into the future with which we are concerned fall at a time when he entered upon his office. Hosea is, as Ewald describes him, the prophet of the highly tragical pain of love. Love contends with wrath until wrath finally disappears in the triumph of love. It is connected with this, so to say, mystic and erotic element of Hosea, that the beginnings of his prophecy are interwoven with two

HOSEA'S VIEW OF THE FINAL PERIOD. 127

marriages, which were commanded him, in order to represent the present and future of Israel in living images. Out of the first prophetic marriage spring three children: Jezreêl, who symbolizes the judgment of destruction, by which the murderous dynasty of Jehu is visited in the plain of Jezreêl; Lo-Ruchâma, whose name indicates that the period of God's grace for the house of Israel is past, while, on the contrary, a wonderful rescue, although not mediated through the power of arms, impends for the house of Judah; and Lo-Ammi, according to whose name Israel has ceased to be God's people, and He may not be Israel's God.

These three children, and the mother of these children, who was originally a prostitute, attest the night side of God's relation to His people. But in chap. ii. this comfortless image of the present is transformed into an image of the future, rich in hopes, since out of the dark ground of the name Lo-Ammi the promise flames forth, that Israel shall be a numerous people, whom Yahweh recognises again as His people and His children; and from the name Jezreêl the promise that again from Judah and Israel there will be one victorious people, under a common head; and from the name Lo-Ruchâma, the promise that the members of this people as such, having found mercy, will mutually welcome each other.

But before the form of the mother clears up, the dark ground of her moral degradation is disclosed. This takes place in ii. 4—15, and with לָכֵן (ver. 16) the transformation of reproof and threatening into the comfort of promise appears; for the reason that now wrath has been poured forth, not without effect (cf. ver. 9*b*), the congregation of Israel receives in the exile Yahweh's sweet persuasive call, and He accompanies them to the wilderness, in the passage between the place of punishment and the land of promise, encouraging those who have become faint through long suffering. From this place the promises begin, which mount higher and higher. The false gods become so thoroughly disagreeable to the congregation that it is dreadful to them to name their names. The entire natural world enters into a covenant of peace with them, and between them and Yahweh there arises a relation of love which has its resemblance in the melting together of two lives in marriage: "And I will espouse thee to me for ever; and I will espouse thee to me in righteousness and justice, and in mercy and in pity. And I will espouse thee to me in truth, and thou shalt recognise the Lord" (את־ה׳).

The dark ground of the congregation, who have given themselves body and soul to idolatry, and who, as such, are typified through Gomer, who was married by the prophet, is now consumed in the absolute brightness of mid-day. Although a higher ascent of the promise from this point is impossible for us, nevertheless it does not rest, but combines before it closes once more the three prophetic forms together with which it began (vers. 23–25): "And it shall come to pass on that day: I will hear, utterance of Yahweh; I will hear the heavens, and these shall hear the earth; and the earth shall hear the corn, and the new wine, and the oil; and these shall hear Jezreêl. And I will sow her [a congregation] to me in the land; and I will have compassion on Lo-Ruchâma, and I will say to Lo-Ammi: 'Thou art my people;' and he shall say: 'My God.'"

The universe is pervaded with the feeling of dependence of one creature upon another; one prays, as it were, to another for the granting of that through which it needs to be supplemented, and this supplication of all creatures is finally a supplication of God, who conditions all things which He makes on a chain of hearing, whose final link is the divine congregation which has been sown in the Holy Land. That which Hosea says here concerning the blessing of the natural world, which descends from heaven as by a ladder, and which speaks of a union of love with God (*unio mystica*), touches Rom. viii. 18-23 and Rev. xix. 6-9, but only from a distance; for all is directed, not to the human race, but to Israel, and not to the earth, but to the land of Israel, which he designates with Jezreêl, as though he meant only the land of the kingdom of Israel. But he means the entire land of promise; for Israel and Judah, as he prophesies (ii. 2*a*), will again be united under one common head. This prophecy in the mouth of the Ephraimitic prophet is more significant than in the mouth of Amos the Judaean. Duhm says:[1] "Hosea, so far as we know, is the first who declares that the continuance of a separate royal house

[1] *Theologie der Propheten*, Bonn 1875, p. 128.

in Israel is unlawful, or better, is sinful, and who categorically demands the abandonment of independence and a return to David." This view of the case is not correct, for all the prophets recognise that the kingdom of Israel exists lawfully; they see in the division of the kingdom a punishment of God which has gone over the house of David, but which will not last for ever: the Israel of the final period will again be one people. But Hosea is indeed the first who gives this hope definite expression, yet more definitely in chap. iii. than in ii. 2, where the prophet, who seems meanwhile to have become a widower, is directed to marry a woman, whose love for him is not her first, so that it is to be feared that the old flame will burn again in her, and threaten the faithfulness of marriage. This wise, strict indeed, but well-meant behaviour of the prophet with this wife who is inclined to adultery, is designed to serve as an image of the dealing which Yahweh adopts with His people, in order to wean them from their infidelity to Him: "For many days the children of Israel shall sit without king, and without prince, and without sacrifice and without statue, and without ephod and teraphim. Afterward shall the children of Israel convert, and seek Yahweh their God, and David their king; and shall come trembling to Yahweh, and to His goodness at the end of the days." This is not a companion-piece to Rom. xi. 25 of the same value. For the Israel of whom Hosea here speaks is Israel in the narrow sense,—the people of the ten tribes,—to which

HOSEA'S VIEW OF THE FINAL PERIOD. 131

he himself belongs. The "many days" is the incalculably long Assyrian exile. The religion of the ten tribes was a state religion, decreed from above (*obenher decretierte*), with the chief places of worship at Bethel and Dan, where the molten images (מַסֵּכָה, 2 Kings xvii. 16), representing Yahweh as a steer stood, and where sacrifices were made to God in the form of a steer, which is indicated by זֶבַח; whereas, on the other hand, מַצֵּבָה designates the statue of Baal (x. 1 f.), and אֵפוֹד וּתְרָפִים (as Judg. xvii. 5) indicate the apparatus of the oracle, by means of which they sought and made known the divine will.

As the prophet removes from his wanton wife her intrigue, so God will remove from His people all the supports and means of promoting an idolatrous worship, especially the government of the state, through which it is seduced to apostasy from the One God, who cannot be represented by an image. In the midst of an exile of long duration, under the pressure of foreign heathenism, and of the condition of punishment into which it is betrayed by its own heathenism, it will be seized by a penitent desire after Yahweh its God and David its king. Those who for centuries have served kings of many dynasties without a promise, will again submit themselves to a king of the house which has the promise of God. Nevertheless דָּוִיד מַלְכָּם will signify more than Reuss says, *la dynastie légitime des Isaïdes*, more than the son of David, ruling precisely at the time when this transformation takes place. It might indeed be thought that this signification of the words would suffice, since Hosea predicts an Assyrian exile, which makes an end of the ten tribes, but not at the same time a Babylonian, through which the Davidic dynasty suffers a breaking off for an incalculably long time. But he knows that also Judah, although a wonderful deliverance awaits it in the time of Assyrian judgment (i. 7), is ripening for a harvest of punishment (vi. 5), and his prophecy has reference to the final period (בְּאַחֲרִית הַיָּמִים), and a king who is indicated not only as מִזֶּרַע דָּוִד or מִבֵּית דָּוִד, but expressly as דָּוִד, can only be such an one in whom David lives again; hence an antitype of David, hence the Messiah, according to which the Targum translates: "They will be obedient to Messiah, the Son of David, their king." The prophecy is Messianic, but its point still remains—the union of Israel with Judah under a second David; and concerning the person of this second David it does not say anything more definite. The connection of the God of Israel and this king allows us only to conclude that he is the anointed of God in full reality.

Remark.—There are also typical elements in the Book of Hosea, but that is not useful material for the reconstruction of the course of development of Messianic prophecy; for, first, when the prophetic text is lighted up by the history of New Testament fulfilment, we shall be surprised by the perception that the word of the prophet here and there, without his knowledge and will, by means of the Spirit of inspiration, takes on a form in which it corresponds to the facts, which are related antitypically to that which was originally intended by them. When Matthew (ii. 15) sees in the fact that Egypt should be a place of refuge for the holy family with the Christ-child, the fulfilment of the word of God in Hos. xi. 1, he certainly does not fail to recognise that that which is said in Hosea is in its first reference intended of Israel; but he does not regard it as a mere accident that as Israel, God's first-born, so also Jesus, God's only born, was concealed for a time in Egypt, and from there, through God's call, returned to the land intended for Him.

Also the prediction of the resurrection of Israel (vi. 1–3) has a typical form. The time will come when the call to repentance will re-echo among the entire people. Israel, in the condition of punishment in which it finds itself, will recognise the judgment of its God, and will have confidence in Him who is not less gracious than just, "for [so they comfort each other] He who hath torn us will heal us, He who smote us will also bind us up. He will make us alive again after two days; on the third day He will raise us up, and we shall live before Him." The people now lies as one dead in the grave, but the second day of his burial will be the turning-point of his new life, and the third day will be the day of his resurrection. As in the bringing back of Israel the יְקִמֵנוּ follows יְחַיֵּנוּ, so in Jesus' breaking through the kingdom of the dead ζωοποίησις, *resuscitatio*, and ἀνάστασις (ἔγερσις), *resurrectio*, are to be discriminated. The resuscitation by means of which spirit and body, released from their unity, secured an independent life, preceded the going forth from the grave in a glorified body.

The history of Israel is, in its great essential

features, an original and copy of the history of Christ. A resurrection day is to follow the two days of the death of Israel, of which the second ends in a transition from death to life. Days of God, not days measured by the sun, are intended, perhaps the Assyrian, the Babylonian, and the Roman exile, in which the Jewish people are still living. Jerome thought that he was compelled to understand Hos. xiii. 14 as treating of the resurrection on account of 1 Cor. xv. 54–57: *Quod apostolus in resurrectionem interpretatus est Domini, nos aliter interpretari nec possumus nec audemus.* But the divine words in Hos. xiii. 14 are not promising, but extremely threatening: " Out of the hand of Hades should I free them, from death should I redeem them ? [no] where are thy plagues, death ? where thy pestilence, O Hades! Pity must be hidden before my eyes." Pity is so near to God, although Israel has so grievously sinned against Him. But now it must depart, in order that He may not be seized by it. He summons against Ephraim, who is hardening itself against Him, Hades and death with the powers of destruction, over which they have control: He suffers this people, without checking them, to fall a prey to Hades and death, so that their bringing again, so far as such a thing is possible, is to be the bringing of one who is dead from his death. Paul does not intend to say by means of 1 Cor. xv. 54 f., τότε γενήσεται ὁ λόγος ὁ γεγραμμένος, that then, when the last enemy is overcome, the Hoseanic expression, ποῦ σου θάνατε κτλ. as prophetic word, is to be fulfilled, but then that will take place which these words of the Old Testament Scriptures, considered as pean (cry of triumph), express.

§ 28. *Isaiah's Fundamental Ideas in their Original Form.*

The activity of Hosea began toward the end of the reign of Jeroboam II., whom Uzziah, according to Biblical chronology, survived about fourteen years. But in the year that Uzziah died—according to Ussher, 758 B.C.; according to Duncker, Wellhausen, and others, 740—Isaiah was called, whose book gives us a deep insight into the gradual development and transformation of his announcement. It is an unhappy calling with which the prophet, raised to heaven in chap. vi., returns to earth. The word which he preaches is to be to his people a savour of death to death, for the time of divine long-suffering is passed. The course of the history of Israel proceeds hereafter through judgment upon judgment in a homeless, distant country, but a remnant remains which is compared to the shoot from the root of a tree which was hewn down. Hitherto there has ruled over Israel the riches of the divine goodness, without their being led to repentance, from this time on God's judging, although not annihilating, but winnowing righteousness. It is the fundamental ideas of his prophecy which Isaiah here receives at his call, in view of the time of judgment through the Assyrian people. From the trisagion of the seraphim he has his favourite designation of God with קְדוֹשׁ יִשְׂרָאֵל. He prophesies that the worldly glory of Israel must be dashed in pieces before the true glory rises on its ruins, connecting with an older prophetic word as the text of his preaching in chaps. ii.–iv., and the appendix (chap. v.), which is developed out of iii. 14.

In the introductory address (chap. i.) which is prefixed to this first cycle of prophecies (chaps. ii.–vi.) it appears that the people of that time are not to be brought back by the way of grace, but only by that of judgment, which melts away the mass of dross in order to release the noble metal which endures the fire.

Here we have the first utterance of the proclamation which is given to the prophet. The world power which becomes God's instrument of punishment appears in v. 26 ff. (cf. Deut. xxviii. 49) before his prophetic eye only, first as a shadowy form without any firm outline. The judgment of the exile is indicated (vi. 12, cf. v. 13) first merely in general expressions. The salvation for which judgment makes way does not proceed further in chap. i. than the modest measure of the return of a better past, as under David, Solomon, and Jehoshaphat. The remnant which is called שְׁאֵרִית or פְּלֵטָה, and which has in Shearyashûb a living emblem, appears first (vi. 13) only in the image of a rooted stock which becomes green again. And the prediction of the time of glory after judgment (iv. 2), where it is said: " On that day the sprout of Yahweh will be for ornament and for glory, and the fruit of the land will be pride and splendour for the escaped of Israel," is yet so general, so clare-obscure, so sketchy, that the discussion as to whether צֶמַח ה' is

ISAIAH'S FUNDAMENTAL IDEAS. 137

intended personally[1] or only as indicating a thing has not yet been closed, and probably will never arrive at a universally recognised result. Briggs still maintains the view, as well as Cheyne and Driver, that the "sprout of Yahweh" and the "fruit of the land" are intended of the endowment of the natural surroundings with an extraordinary beauty and fruitfulness. On the contrary, von Orelli,[2] Bredenkamp, Schultz[3] recognise that the expression of the high self-consciousness, so far as it was warranted at that time, sounds too grand to have only things of the natural world as its object. The picture concerning the fall of false glory contains nothing to which this natural glory (as in John iv. 18) could, on the other hand, be related. Nevertheless, it must be admitted that פְּרִי הָאָרֶץ, which is parallel to צֶמַח יְהוָה, is rather contradictory to the personal understanding than favourable to it. Hence by the sprout and fruit we are not to understand points of light, but circles of light,—the divine gifts and blessings of which the Israel of the future could boast. But it ever remains established that it is this circle of light out of which as its centre, as God's "unspeakable gift" (ἀνεκδιήγητος δωρεά, 2 Cor. ix. 14), the Messiah enters into the consciousness of the prophets.

---

[1] It is thus understood by the Targum, which translates it משיחא די"י, while the Septuagint adopts an entirely different text.

[2] *Der Prophet Jesaia*, Erlangen 1887, p. 25.

[3] *Alttestamentliche Theologie*, Göttingen 1889, p. 776.

138 MESSIANIC PROPHECIES IN HISTORICAL SUCCESSION.

§ 29. *The Great Trilogy of Messianic Prophecies,
Isa. vii., ix., xi.*

I. IMMANUEL, THE SON OF THE VIRGIN.

In chaps. vii.–xii. the history of the time takes on another form. Towards the end of the reign of Jotham the hostilities had begun which occasioned the formation of the league between Syria and Ephraim for the purpose of overthrowing the dynasty of David (2 Kings xv. 37). Rezin, the king of Damascene Syria, took possession of the harbour Elath, which Uzziah had taken from the Edomites (2 Kings xvi. 6; cf. xiv. 22). The Judaeans, who had settled there, were carried captive to Damascus (2 Chron. xxviii. 5). And Ahaz was conquered by Pekah, the king of Israel, in a fearfully bloody battle, after which the prophet Oded rescued the numerous Judaean prisoners from the disgrace of slavery (2 Chron. xxviii. 6–15). The armies of the allies after they had conquered separately were now united and prepared for the main attack on Jerusalem. In the midst of the danger, which had reached its highest point, Isaiah appeared with his son Shearyashûb before the king, who was at that time on the west side of the city engaged in making arrangements with reference to the approaching siege, and promised him God's help, offering Ahaz any kind of a sign that he might demand. There is scarcely a Biblical fact to which supernaturalism could so appeal as to this in order to support its lawful claim against the modern view of the world. The prophet knows that the God in him is the God of grace in whose being it lies to prove Himself a power exalted above nature, and that the God of grace whom he serves is the God of miraculous power, who, when the ends of the history of redemption demand it, can make the laws of nature serviceable to these ends. But Ahaz does not wish to have any trial made of the help of Yahweh. He has already summoned the help of Tiglath-Pileser, king of Asshur, and with hypocritical pretences rejects the offer of Isaiah.

This scene is one of the most momentous crises in the history of Israel. The summoning of the help of Asshur through Ahaz laid the foundation for that complication with the world empire which in 722 B.C. brought destruction to the kingdom of Israel, and in 588 B.C. to the kingdom of Judah, unable to change the unfortunate beginning of the king; and, on the other hand, certain of this, that the promise of God given to the house of David could not be brought to nought by any human interference contrary to the will of God, the prophet replies that the Lord Himself will give them—the king and his house—a sign contrary to their own choice (vii. 13–17): "Hear now, house of David! Is it too little for you to weary men, that ye weary also my God? therefore the Almighty Himself will give you a sign: Behold the maiden is with child, and bears a son, and calls his name Immanuel. Butter and honey shall he eat at the time when he shall understand[1] to reject the evil and choose the good. For before the boy shall understand to reject the evil and choose the good, the land shall be desolate, before whose two kings thou art terribly afraid. Yahweh will bring upon thee and thy people and thy father's house days, such as have not been since the day when Ephraim tore away from Judah, the king of Asshur."

A nameless maid or virgin—as we have a right to translate it with the Septuagint, since הָעַלְמָה certainly indicates a young woman who had not yet become a mother—whom God has chosen and His Spirit has made present to the prophet, shall bear the One in whom God will be the help of His people, and whose continuance will be assured[2] through the judgments which are in prospect.

The birth of this Immanuel is the אוֹת [sign] worked by God, which takes the place of the sign which Ahaz declined to ask. The meeting of Isaiah with Ahaz occurred about the year 734 B.C., and it is impossible

[1] Not, in order that he may understand (learn) to distinguish between the good and the evil, so that the desolation of the land may be the means ordained by God "for the intellectual development of Immanuel" (Guthe, *Zukunftsbild*, p. 40). If that were the meaning, then לְדַעַת should be said (cf. *e.g.* l. 4, לדעת, not לדעתו).

[2] We can say that Isaiah is the prophet of the אוֹת, for a characteristic trait of the prophet is the אוֹת, the sign, consisting in predicted facts (vii. 14, xxxvii. 30), or deeds accomplished at the present time (xxxviii. 22, 7, cf. vii. 11), or symbolical representations (xx. 3, viii. 18). He is the prophet who stands security for the future through wonders in word and deed.

TRILOGY OF MESSIANIC PROPHECIES. 141

that the sign can first have been realized after seven centuries: the birth of Immanuel is in the view of the prophet a fact of the immediate future. For he sees the help which is mediated by Immanuel dawn in the following directions on every side: (1) Damascene Syria and the Ephraimitish kingdom are conquered by Asshur,—externally considered, brought about indeed through Ahaz' politics, but an event known before by God and received into His plan; (2) but then Asshur turns against the Israel of both kingdoms, and the land is overflowed by the armies of Asshur and Egypt, the two great powers who are rivals, and is desolated to such an extent that it becomes a great pasture, and the nourishment of the poor thin population is reduced to milk and honey—at this time of misery, for which Ahaz is responsible, falls, according to the view of the prophet, the growth of Immanuel, who, even when he has outgrown the years of childhood (Deut. i. 39), must content himself with the monotonous nourishment of the reduced wild country.

Those who think that Immanuel, because he was a child of the Assyrian time of judgment, could not be the Messiah, fail to recognise the law of perspective shortening to which all prophecy, even that concerning Jesus Christ Himself in the Gospels, is subject. Isaiah lived to see that the expectation of the parousia of the Messiah in the time of the Assyrian oppression was not fulfilled; nevertheless he was not ashamed of his prophecy, and did not withdraw it. For as Asshur suffered wreck on Jerusalem, he knew that this had not occurred without the co-operation of the promised Immanuel, who was not yet born, to whom, praying for help (viii. 8), he looks up: " The spreading of the pinions of Asshur fill the breadth of thy land, Immanuel!" The future One, although he has not yet appeared possessed of a body, leads an ideal life in the Old Testament history; and as he appeared in the fulness of the times, the holy land, not indeed under the foreign dominion of Asshur, but under that of Rome, was in a condition which went back to the untheocratic politics of Ahaz as its ultimate cause.[1]

And he is not born in a palace and wrapped in purple, not an "alma" of the harem (Cant. vi. 8) of the Davidic king was his mother, but the betrothed of a carpenter from the reduced family of David, who recognised him as his legitimate though not corporeal son, but as a gift of heaven. The modern theology sees in it a myth spun out of Isa. vii. 14; we see in it with the entire Church of God the fulfilment and unriddling of the Isaianic word of prophecy.

---

[1] In relation to this idea is the representation that according to liii. 2a he sprouts as "a root out of a dry ground." Even when he comes into the world he has to suffer the consequences of the sin of his people, but only with them, so that in this feature of the portrait of the Messiah by Isaiah there is only to be seen from far, as George Adam Smith maintains, a beginning of a representation of a suffering Messiah.

§ 30. *The Great Trilogy of Messianic Prophecies, Isa. vii., ix., xi.*

II. THE BEGINNING OF A NEW PERIOD WITH THE NEW HEIR OF THE DAVIDIC THRONE.

Isaiah does not say expressly, in chap. vii., what the son of the virgin, who grows up in the land which is deeply sunken, through the fault of the house of David at that time, will do for the people and the land; only the signification of the name Immanuel (with us is God) indicates it. In chap. viii. the prediction begun in vii. 17 concerning the oppression of Asshur is continued. Like the shoreless Euphrates, Asshur overflows the land of Ephraim and then of Judah. Praying for help the prophet calls on Immanuel, as if exhorting him, that he should hasten his work of deliverance, which his name indicates. This view, directed to the future One, and to God, who in him will be the stay of His people, is immediately transformed (viii. 9 f.) into the triumphant confidence of a granted petition. But that which faith anticipates lies at the time only in the range of the future. The night must first come on the people who have forgotten God, but a night upon which there follows a dawn for those who gather together for the sake of the prophetic word of God, although only for these; and the parts of the northern boundary which have received the severest visitation, and which, for this reason, are most susceptible to God's gracious interference, are first privileged to see the great light which breaks through the dark shadow of death. Israel, after it has been blended together to a remnant, and becomes a numerous people, happy through victory and blessing, free from the yoke of the oppressor, and bloody war will have an end; " for "—continues the prophet, referring the glorious period of restoration back to him with whom and through whom it comes—" a child is born to us, a son is given to us, and the government lies upon his shoulder, and they call his name: Wonderful, Counsellor, Strong God, Eternal Father, Prince of Peace; of the increase of his government and peace there shall be no end, to order it and to establish it upon David's throne and over his kingdom through judgment and righteousness from this time forth and for ever: the zeal of Yahweh of hosts will perform this."

The predicted son of the virgin is now born, and the prophet, since his ideal life is continued in the future, greets and celebrates him as the heir to the Davidic throne. It is a fivefold name which he bears. He is, according to vii. 14, a wonderful sign and a wonderful gift. For this reason, therefore, we do not combine פֶּלֶא יוֹעֵץ in one name, which would signify, not one who was a prodigy of a counsellor,— for which Gen. xvi. 12, Prov. xxi. 20, does not furnish any similar example,—but would signify one counselling wonderful things, one counselling wonderfully. There are two names. He is called פֶּלֶא, as a divinely-

TRILOGY OF MESSIANIC PROPHECIES. 145

wrought prodigy[1] in person. It is evident that we must combine this name, as first with vii. 14, because even here the veil of secrecy lies upon his birth. He must be a son of David, since he takes the Davidic throne; and since the family in a genealogical sense is determined by the father and not by the mother, he must be the legitimate son of a descendant of David; but the prophecy says nothing about a corporeal father. And we are further justified in combining the name אֵל גִּבּוֹר with the name עִמָּנוּאֵל. We are to explain this name, not according to Ezek. xxxii. 21, where אֵלֵי גִבּוֹרִים indicates the mightiest among the heroes (cf. Ezek. xxxi. 11), but according to Isa. x. 21, where, as in all other places, it is the name of God, the Strong One. But for this reason we do not mean that the Old Testament prophet, whose image of the Messiah does not yet burst the frame of the royal image, connected with this name of the Messiah a metaphysical, or, in any wise, a Nicene dogmatic signification, only that he regards this king as God of the strong bodily present: God is in him, he is God the Strong One, as the Angel of Yahweh is Yahweh Himself. And we do not explain the name אֲבִי־עַד, like Schultz and others, as father of prey; for עַד expresses in such genitive connections, where they otherwise occur (xlv. 17, cf. lvii. 15; Hab. iii. 6, cf. Gen. xlix. 26), the attribute of eternity; and the

[1] It is also more probable that there are five names—a half *dekas*—not four, for the sake of the Biblical symbolism of numbers.

prophecy says further that he shall possess the throne of David for ever, without transmitting it; that in a righteous and peaceful rule he shall enlarge his dominion; that, therefore, he shall be an eternal Father, that is, loving and beloved of a great people. The names יוֹעֵץ and שַׂר־שָׁלוֹם indicate him also as ruler; the former, as such an one in whom the people could have full confidence; the latter, as such an one whose exalted activity has peace as its object. It is significant that the fivefold name, as the threefold Aaronitic blessing, ends in שָׁלוֹם, of all gifts that which makes most happy and is most desired.

Although, indeed, this Isaianic image of the Messiah, in order to have a New Testament value, must be removed from the Old Testament national narrowness (for the king of the kingdom of heaven is king of Israel, not in a special sense, but in none other than that in which he is king of all the nations), nevertheless, the three Messianic predictions of the Messiah contain not only ideal, but also historical features, which are strengthened as essential through the history of fulfilment. The second as well as the first hides the birth of the future One in mysterious obscurity, and the second testifies that Galilee shall first behold the Messiah, according to which it became Jewish tradition that the Messiah should first be revealed in Galilee, and that from Tiberias the time of the redemption of Israel would dawn.[1]

[1] See *Ein Tag in Kapernaum*, p. 20.

§ 31. *The Great Trilogy of Messianic Prophecies,*
Isa. vii., ix., xi.

III. CHARACTERISTICS OF THE SECOND DAVID AND OF HIS GOVERNMENT.

The Isaianic addresses in chaps. vii.–xii., as even the new beginnings which are repeated show (וַיֹּאמֶר ה׳, vii. 3, viii. 1; וַיּוֹסֶף ח׳ דַּבֵּר, viii. 5; דָּבָר שָׁלַח אֲדֹנָי), are not one whole, from one smelting, and from the same time. The standpoint of the prophet brings the invasion of Asshur, announced in vii. 17, nearer and nearer. In chap. x. he describes prophetically how the Assyrian army advances continually against Jerusalem, spreading terror; and how, like a wood with lofty branches planted against it, through the terrible power of the divine manifestation of glory, it is dashed together to the ground. But while the Lebanon of the world-power is broken in pieces, the house of David, which has become like the stump (*truncus*) of a felled tree, renews its youth (xi. 1): "And there goes forth [perfect of result] a twig from the stump of Jesse, and a shoot from its roots bears fruit."

The prediction here goes back to the birth of the son and heir of David's throne, celebrated in ix. 5 f. The twig which springs from the stump of the house of David, which has sunk down to the lowliness of its Bethlehemitish origin, is the son of David who is hoped for, who, with himself and through himself, raises his people from lowliness to glory. The Lord acknowledges him and sets him apart, and endows him with the entire sevenfold fulness of His Spirit (ver. 2): "And there sinks down upon him the Spirit of Yahweh, spirit of wisdom and understanding, spirit of counsel and of might, spirit of knowledge and of the fear of Yahweh." The calling for which he is prepared, since the Spirit of God in the entire richness of its powers becomes his possession, is the royal one, with its duties as ruler and judge (vers. 3–5): "And the fear of Yahweh is perfume to him; and not according to that which his eyes see does he judge, and not according to that which his ears hear [not according to sensuous appearances, but according to actual facts and the condition of the heart] does he speak judgment: and he judges with righteousness the poor, and speaks judgment with equity for the meek of the land; and smites the earth with the rod of his mouth, and with the breath of his lips he slays the wicked. And righteousness is the girdle of his loins, and fidelity is the girdle of his hips." He is a king according to God's heart, and of divine power, who is here described. "And he smites the earth" (ver. 4*b*) is a superhuman feature in the image; but every feature of redemptive history is wanting. From this king to one who redeems the earth from the bondage of sin and the curse of death it is still a long way. But the history of fulfilment shows that also this prophecy is a work of the Spirit of God in the laboratory of the spirit of the prophet. The one described is king, but not acquirer and communicator of spiritual benefits, hence more Christ than Jesus. But was not Jesus the designated King of the kingdom of heaven, as He took upon Himself the baptism of the claim to the kingdom of heaven?[1] And is it not a transposition of prophecy in history that the Holy Spirit comes down upon the One ascending from the water in the form of a dove, that is, in the soft manner and in the entire fulness of His being, and that then, as He enters upon His office, not immediately as king, but first as prophet of the kingdom of heaven, the first words of His mouth have reference to the poor, the burden bearers, the meek, hence the דַּלִּים and עַנְוֵי־אָרֶץ, and raise these up by means of promises? On the contrary, the destruction of the final arch-enemy of Christ and His kingdom, which Paul (2 Thess. ii. 8) predicts with the words of Isaiah (xi. 4b), is still a fact, which no comparison of the history with that which is predicted justifies. The same is true of the prediction of the future paradisiacal peace of nature, which will accompany, mirror, and complete the peaceful rule of the second David (xi. 6–9). The prophet establishes this transformation of the animal world on the fact that the earth shall then be full of the knowledge of the God of salvation as the bottom of the sea is overflowed with water. The peaceful condition of the animal world with reference to each other and to mankind is not therefore limited here, as in Hos. ii. 20, to Israel and his land, but is extended to the earth and to mankind; but it can only be understood under the presupposition that the prophet beholds the glorious

[1] German, "*Anwartschaft auf das Himmelreich.*"

conclusion of the earthly history in connection with the glorified new earth. The case is different with xi. 10: "And it shall come to pass on that day that the root of Jesse, which stands as a banner of the peoples, after it shall the nations inquire, and his resting-place [that is, the place where he dwells and thrones] is glory." This has been fulfilled to the extent that, since Christianity has entered into the world, at least a third of the heathen world has flocked about the cross of the Christ who has been glorified through suffering.

Hence, therefore, this great prophecy (xi. 1–10) may be divided into three parts: (1) That which awaits a fulfilment, which therefore cannot be controlled; (2) that which is limited to the nation, and which as political is external, which both requires a New Testament enlargement and a spiritual deepening; and (3) that which has been literally fulfilled, which shows that what has been predicted is the word of God, even although it is in the form of contemporary history.

Remark.—In the New Testament only the Gospel of Matthew refers to the first three Isaianic images of the Messiah, which (i. 22 f.) designates the miracle of the birth of Jesus as a fulfilment of Isa. vii. 14. The miracle is also narrated by Luke; but although more fully than by Matthew, yet without reference to the prophetic word of Isaiah. Paul also merely says (Gal. iv. 4) that God in the fulness of time sent forth His Son, born of a woman. He does not say born of a virgin, nor do we expect it; the connection of thought in the passage excludes such a reference as not to be expected. But that he had the miraculous nature of the birth in mind appears, nevertheless, to be implied from a comparison of his words, "His Son," "born of a woman," with Luke i. 35. Isaiah's second Messianic image remains in the New Testament without any application. It is never cited in order to establish the deity of Christ by means of it. The Septuagint could not be used for this purpose, for they translate the Hebrew words פֶּלֶא יוֹעֵץ אֵל after another reading by μεγάλης βουλῆς ἄγγελος; cf. in connection with this what we have said in § 22 concerning the mediating angel in the Book of Job. On the contrary, the third image of the Messiah is again mirrored many fold in the New Testament. Matthew refers in ii. 23 to Isa. xi. 1 when he says, that thus should be fulfilled what the prophet had said that the future Christ should be called a Nazarene, that is, one from Nazareth, because Joseph settled with the child Jesus in Nazareth. Even Jerome remarks on Isa. xi. 1 that *eruditi Hebraei* have this passage of the Book of Isaiah in mind concerning the fruitful נֵצֶר from the root of Jesse. He certainly does not cite one prophet, but the prophets. He thinks at the same time of Isa. liii. and other passages, according to which it is barren land out of which the future One is to grow, and that he will appear with an insignificant exterior. He sees the image of נֵצֶר embodied in connection with the image of the shoot from the root (liii. 2) and other prophetic words which speak of the ignoring and despising of the future One, since insignificant Nazareth, lying at a distance from Jerusalem, in despised Galilee, became the ground upon which Jesus grew, so that in the mouth of the people He was depreciatingly called הַנָּצְרִי.[1] This is the most probable, nevertheless the account remains a riddle. From the statement concerning the sevenfold spirit which rests upon the second David, are taken the seven spirits (ἑπτὰ πνεύματα) of the Revelation (i. 4), which appear (iv. 5) as seven torches before God's throne, and as the seven eyes of the Lamb (v. 6). The prediction concerning the destruction of the רָשָׁע (Isa. xi. 4b) is brought by Paul into the more special connection of redemptive history (2 Thess. ii. 8), and the figure of the staff of his mouth is embodied in vision (Rev. i. 16). The designation of Christ as the true and faithful witness (Rev. i. 5, iii. 14) is connected with Isa. xi. 5b; while, on the other hand, the designation ὁ 'Ἀμήν (Rev. iii. 14) may be compared with אֱלֹהֵי אָמֵן (Isa. lxv. 16), and is occasioned through the Lord's ordinary formula of assertion, ἀμὴν λέγω ὑμῖν (אָמֵן אֲמֵינָא לְכוֹן). But the name ἡ ῥίζα Δαυίδ, which is given Him in Rev. v. 5, xxii. 16, is the same as שֹׁרֶשׁ יִשַׁי (Isa. xi. 10).

§ 32. *The Son of God in Ps.* ii.

As Isaiah, praying for help, looks on high to Immanuel (Isa. viii. 8), in whom Yahweh will be the support of His people, he immediately receives the assurance that he is heard; and as he combines with

---

[1] He is also called נצר in *Bereshith rabba*. One of the alleged four apostles also has the same designation in the Talmud. Although the Talmudists mention a number of Palestinian places, yet they observe a deep silence with regard to Nazareth.

Asshur all the peoples who storm against God's people, he pronounces upon them the judgment of being crushed and broken in pieces, and summons all the ends of the earth to take warning from this judgment. The first group of verses (1-5) of the anonymous second Psalm contains much the same. The poet, who lives in a time when the throne of David is tottering, is transported for the comfort of himself and his contemporaries into the future, where all the nations of the world shall rebel against Yahweh and His Christ (מְשִׁיחוֹ), but without being able to accomplish anything against God's immovable order. Yahweh's address in His anger forms the beginning of the second group of verses (6–9), and without introduction, as in a drama, there follows immediately the address of His Christ. The address of Yahweh begins with וַאֲנִי, as in Isa. vii. 14 with וְאַתֶּם. The sentence which continues with "and," since the address storms, is swallowed up in the contrast: "[Ye rebel against me], and yet [in the perfection of my power] I have set my king upon Zion my holy mountain"—the rebellion against the divine king is therefore rebellion against God Himself. And now follows the address of the king, which is designed to proclaim with what words of highest honour and world-embracing power Yahweh has chosen and promoted him: "I will make proclamation concerning a decree [it designedly sounds so circumstantial and official]: Yahweh said to me: Thou art my son, this day have I begotten thee. Ask of me, and I will give thee nations for thy inheritance, and the ends of the earth for thy possession. Thou shalt break them in pieces [the Septuagint, Rev. xii. 5, xix. 15, without any essential difference in meaning: feed] with a rod of iron, thou shalt dash them in pieces as a potter's vessel." The expression to-day (היּוֹם) is certainly not intended of the day of birth into this earthly existence; for that a father should say concerning his son on the day of his birth that he begat him on the same day, is meaningless. It is true that by לְדִתִּיךָ a supersensuous power exalted above the begetting of the father and the bearing of the mother is intended; but the expression sounds human, and is therefore opposed to the meaning which, regarded with reference to the relation of father and son, is not true to nature, and therefore would be contrary to nature. There is therefore intended a begetting, not in the earthly, but in the royal existence, as the term "to-day" is understood by Paul (Acts xiii. 33, cf. Rom. i. 4), since it refers to the *dies regalis* of the resurrection; for the resurrection of Jesus, the Christ, was a transporting from the life in the form of a servant to the royal life of glorification and exaltation at the right hand of the Father. The Old Testament does not indeed distinguish between the birth in the earthly and the birth in the heavenly existence. But to a certain extent Isaiah makes the distinction, since he first celebrates the birth of the royal child (ix. 5 f.), and later his royal consecration (cf. Acts x. 33) and royal rule.

The third and last group of verses of the psalm

SON OF GOD IN SECOND PSALM.

infers from that which the spirit of prophecy brought before the poet and seer, earnest warnings for the rulers of the earth (vers. 10–12): "And now kings, receive understanding, be admonished, rulers of the earth. Serve the Lord with fear, and rejoice [because of the happiness of being permitted to be the servant of such a God] with trembling [in order not to fall into irreverence, security, and arrogance]. Kiss the son, lest he [namely, Yahweh, the Father of this son] be angry and ye perish; for His anger easily burns,—blessed are those who hide in Him."

The following considerations are in favour of the translation of נַשְּׁקוּ־בַר, "kiss the son:" (1) that this designation of the anointed is fittingly introduced, after Yahweh has called him בְּנִי; (2) that the omission of the article need not surprise us. The word is used, like עֶלְיוֹן, תְּהוֹם, תֵּבֵל, as a proper name. It is an Aramaism, such as poetry is fond of (cf. the Aramaism אֶרְחָמְךָ, "I love thee," with which Ps. xviii. begins); here it is probable, because the expression נַשְּׁקוּ בֶן בֶּן would not be euphonious; (3) "kissing" as an expression of allegiance corresponds to an ancient custom, not the kissing of the mouth, but the kissing of the feet, as frequently in the Assyrian inscriptions, and on the part of the woman (Luke vii. 38). Only one thing could seem to be adduced against the expression "kiss the son:" not one of the ancient Greek, Latin, or Syrian translators found this meaning in the words. Even Aquila, Symmachus, Jerome, who recognise the meaning of adoration as implied in נַשְּׁקוּ, translate בר

as an adverb: "Kiss with pure feeling" (Jerome: *adorate pure*). But all of the attempts to translate בר differently than in the sense of son do not weigh, for they are all contrary to the use of the language. It is to be urged against Hitzig and Hupfeld, who translate נַשְּׁקוּ, "submit yourselves" (the former: "to duty;" the latter: "sincerely"), that perhaps the Kal of the verb can signify: "Submit yourselves" (cf. Gen. xli. 40); but it is impossible that the Piel should have this signification. Hence Luther's translation, "Kiss the son," is justified irrefutably. This second psalm belongs to the most important Christological documents. It is not only because here the ideal king of the final period is called מָשִׁיחַ, also the name of the Messiah as God's Son secures here, compared with the general character of the promise (2 Sam. vii.), individual definiteness. The Midrash to the psalm places Ps. ii. 7 and Dan. vii. 13 in reciprocal relations. The self-designations of the Lord with υἱὸς τοῦ θεοῦ and υἱὸς τοῦ ἀνθρώπου, stand in undeniable relation to these Old Testament passages, although they do not have their roots in it, and in the conception which they present are not to be limited by them.

§ 33. *The Messianic Elements in the Addresses of Isa.* xiv. 24–xxxix.

We should be in error if we regarded the three great Messianic prophecies in chaps. vii.–xii. as a continuation which belongs to the time of Ahaz, so that all three have the unhappy government of Ahaz as a dark foil; and it would be a false conclusion if we were to infer from this that Messianic prophecy is so bound to the law of contrast, that for this reason during the better reign of Hezekiah it entirely or almost entirely ceased.

The first Messianic image is from the time of Ahaz, before help was given by Tiglath-Pileser; the second, likewise from the time of Ahaz, shortly before the chastisement of Ephraim (734 B.C.) and of Damascus (732 B.C.); but the third, as appears from x. 9–11, is from the time after the fall of Samaria (722 B.C.), and hence from the beginning of the time of Hezekiah— later than his sixth year, which, according to Biblical chronology, was the year of the fall of Samaria. Messianic prophecy, therefore, describes in the time from Ahaz to Hezekiah its ecliptic, and reaches its high-noon under Hezekiah, since at that time the rising of the kingdom of the Messiah is contrasted with the setting of the world-empire. If we remember this, we shall not seek after an explanation of the fact, that after chap. xi. no Messianic image meets us which corresponds to the three in greatness; and, on the other hand, in the case of those passages whose Messianic meaning is doubtful, we shall not deny a Messianic sense, under the influence of a preconceived false opinion.

When, in the prediction against Philistia (Isa. xiv. 29), it is said, that out of the root of the serpent a basilisk shall go forth, and that the fruit of this shall be a flying dragon, we may consider it as possible that the שָׂרָף מְעוֹפֵף is an image of the Messiah as a punitive power who is to be feared by Philistia (cf. Isa. xi. 14).

The probability of a Messianic meaning is still greater with regard to the foundation-stone in Zion (Isa. xxviii. 16). In the passage xxviii., xxix.–xxxii., we get a deep view into the time of Hezekiah, which seeks to restore what the time of Ahaz has destroyed. But the politics is now still more worldly than theocratic. Ahaz leaned upon Asshur against Syria and Ephraim, and now they seek to shake off the yoke of Asshur with the help of Egypt. Isaiah follows this projected alliance from the time that it is hatched, through all the stages of its development, with his annihilating criticism. In chap. xxviii., which is from the time before the fall of Samaria, he prophesies that the deceptive hope will be brought to shame, and places (ver. 16) in contrast with the fleshly ground of confidence a better one: " For therefore, saith the Almighty Yahweh: Behold, I am He who lays in Zion a stone, a stone of preservation, a precious cornerstone of well-founded foundation—the believer does not flee," that is, has in this stone foundation firmness and support. This stone is not Zion, for it is laid in Zion, and not Yahweh, since He has laid it, but the Davidic kingdom, enduring for ever, according to the promise; but not as a foundation in itself, for an irreconcilable abstraction cannot comfort and encourage; hence it is connected, in thought, with the person of a possessor, but not of the possessor at that time; for Hezekiah, although he was a pious king, was also to blame for the danger of destruction which was threatened by Asshur; but it is connected, in thought, with a promised possessor,—with a divine Retreat and Deliverer whom the Lord will present to His people.

This prophecy is therefore a fourth image of the Messiah; an emblematical image, which is to be understood according to the three direct personal ones, and is thus understood in Rom. ix. 33; 1 Pet. ii. 6 f.

On the contrary, it is not the Messiah who is intended in Isa. xxxii. 1: "Behold, according to righteousness the king (מֶלֶךְ, without the article) shall rule, and the commanders, according to justice shall they command." Likewise xxxiii. 17: "The king (מֶלֶךְ) in his beauty thine eyes shall behold; shall see a free land far away." The Messiah is the king who concludes the history of Israel; but in both these passages a king who continues the history is intended. The standpoint of the prophet is different here from what it is in xi. 1. There he sees, immediately after the catastrophe of Asshur, the glory of the Messianic kingdom arise; but here he speaks from the perception, which he has secured meanwhile, that the catastrophe of Asshur which is given him to predict will indeed be a wonderful revenge and rescue, but yet not the annihilation of Asshur, and not at all the annihilation of the world-empire.

But of the same rank with the three, or four, images of the Messiah, since it is not less of a New Testament character, is the future image which forms the conclusion of the oracle concerning Egypt (Isa. xix.), the second half of which we are not compelled by any sufficient or stringent reasons to regard as the continuation of the first Isaianic by a later prophet. That which is said in Isa. xix. 24 f. sounds like Paul. Old Testament prophecy here does its utmost; for it is not an incorporation of the heathen who are converted among the people of God which is here hoped for, but a brotherly bond between Israel and the nations upon the basis of equal rights. "In that day Israel shall be a third part with Egypt and Asshur, a blessing in the midst of the earth, since Yahweh blesses it, saying: Blessed art thou, my people Egypt, and thou, the work of my hands, Asshur, and thou, mine heir Israel." In the truly humane words of Solomon (1 Kings viii. 43), Israel still remains, in distinction from the other peoples, God's people; but here the name of God's people has lost its exclusiveness, and the spirit of revelation places in prospect before the religion of revelation the future abolition of national exclusiveness.

§ 34. *The Elements of Progress in Micah's Messianic Proclamation.*

Micah began his ministry under Jotham. His book begins with the threatening of Samaria and Jerusalem. It is a brief compilation, composed before 722 B.C., of that which he preached from the time of Jotham until about the sixth year of Hezekiah (cf. Jer. xxvi. 18 f.). If we pass by the doubtful addresses of Isaiah, his view of the distant future reaches farther than Isaiah's. The latter prophesies (Isa. xxxix. 5 ff.) that the riches and the members of the house of David, in the time after Hezekiah, will migrate to Babylon, and will be given into the hand of the king of Babylon. He foresees, therefore, the future world-dominion of Babylon, and the Babylonian exile, beginning with the house of the king. Micah, however, not only prophesies the Babylonian exile, but also the deliverance from it (iv. 10): "Writhe and cast forth [namely, the burden of the body, with which the burden of sorrow is compared; therefore: give thyself up to thy pain, and let it have free course], for at length thou must go out from the fortified city, and encamp upon the field and come to Babylon—there thou shalt be rescued, there Yahweh will redeem thee from the hand of thine enemies."[1]

We remark, in opposition to those who think that these prophecies of both prophets, although they mutually confirm each other, appear to go too far, and are improbable, that the progress of Micah beyond Isaiah is evident in other respects; for while Isaiah (xi. 1) sees the time of Messianic glory and peace dawn immediately after the crash of Asshur, in view of the miraculous deliverance of Jerusalem, it dawns in Micah immediately after the destruction of Jerusalem

[1] The reading ἐκ Βαβυλῶνος of the Septuagint, in iv. 8, is a gloss which has crept in from this passage.

through the world-power, for he threatens (iii. 12):
" Therefore on your account Zion shall be thrown down
to a field, and Jerusalem shall become heaps of ruins,
and the mountain of the temple wooded heights;" and
thus, after the threatening has reached its utmost depth
and has exhausted itself, it is transformed, since it is
no longer kept back by anything, into promise (iv. 1):
" And it shall come to pass at the end of the days:
that the mountain of Yahweh shall be lifted up to the
summit of the mountains and raised above the hills,
and peoples shall stream unto it." It is this prophecy
which Isaiah, ii. 1–4, prefixes, as a derived text, to
his threatening address concerning the overthrow of
worldly glory, which perhaps also in Micah, as the
abrupt beginning (ver. 5) seems to indicate, is taken
from the prophecy of an older prophet—perhaps Joel
—concerning the final elevation of the mountain of
the house of Yahweh, concerning the migration of the
peoples desiring salvation to it, and concerning the
transformation of the murderous implements of war
into the peaceful implements of agriculture; for the
same reason in Micah and Isaiah: " for from Zion
shall go forth a torah (divine revelation), and a word of
Yahweh from Jerusalem "—in the history of fulfilment,
" the gospel of peace " (Eph. vi. 15). The final period,
into which the prophet further sees, is the time of
the bringing of the diaspora of Israel (Micah iv. 6), the
completion of the dominion of Yahweh (ver. 7), the
restoration of the Davidic kingdom (ver. 8), the rescue
from the Babylon whither the people, powerless against

its enemies, shall be driven (ver. 9 f.), the visitation of punishment on the hardened mass of the peoples who storm the restored Zion (vers. 11-13),—the prophet arranges these events of the final period, not according to the chronology, but according to his connection of thought, which is determined through the ethical purpose,—by עַתָּה, which is as remarkably frequent in Micah as in Hosea, he fixes points partly of the farther, partly of the nearer future. The word עַתָּה (ver. 14) is in the same category with עַתָּה (ver. 9)—it fixes a point of the nearer future, a part of the tribulations preceding the salvation and the glory: " Now gather thyself together, daughter of the warlike host [that is, concentrate thyself for mutual counsel, comfort, protection, otherwise so fond of war and courageous in battle]: he [Asshur] threatens us with siege, they smite with the stick upon the cheek of the ruler of Israel." Micah prophesies in the time of Assyrian judgment. According to Isa. x. 24, xxx. 31, smiting with the stick seems to be characteristic of the behaviour of Asshur. The king whom they smite upon the cheek is the opposite of the " king in his beauty," that is, the One who has passed away beyond dishonourable treatment (Isa. xxxiii. 17). The destiny which immediately impends over Israel, is to be shamefully, and without rescue, surrendered to the world-empire.

But the prophet now contrasts with this picture of humiliation the picture of exaltation, which the second David, proceeding from Bethlehem, brings to his people: "And thou Bethlehem Ephrâtah, too small to be reckoned among the districts of Judah,[1] out of thee shall he go forth to me who shall be ruler over Israel; and his goings forth are from antiquity, from the days of the primitive time." Why from Bethlehem? There is the house of David's family, from which the divine election of grace brought him forth (1 Sam. xvi. 1), and made out of the shepherd of sheep a shepherd of Israel. If the divine ruler is born there, and not in the royal city Jerusalem, the Davidic royal house is reduced to its root, and from it renews its youth (Isa. xi. 1, 10).

"The coming to Babylon" (Micah iv. 10) involves in itself, indeed, a violent rupture of the Davidic chain of rulers. But God's power and grace restore the "ancient rule" (Micah iv. 8), and in a king whose origin, on the one hand, is a lowly and unnoticeable one, but on the other hand dates back to the hoary antiquity (cf. on the expression Micah vii. 14, 20); for he whose cradle would be insignificant Bethlehem is the king at whom the divine decree of the promise aimed, ever since it expressed the royal dominion of the people of

---

[1] The citation (Matt. ii. 5) forsakes the Septuagint, which reads אֶפְרָתָה, and בְּאַלְפֵי like the traditional text, and translates freely: "And thou Bethlehem, land of Judah (בֵּית לֶחֶם אֶרֶץ יְהוּדָה), art by no means the smallest among the princes (בְּאַלְפֵי) of Judah"—for the smallness of Bethlehem and the greatness of its mission are contrasted. It is not improbable that the evangelist in this passage follows an old Targum. The originality of the two לִהְיוֹת is assured through the double τοῦ εἶναι of the Septuagint.

Abraham. From the fact that the future One shall come from Bethlehem a retrospective conclusion is drawn: "Therefore he will then give them up, until the time that she that travaileth hath brought forth, and the remnant of his brethren together (עַל, with, as in Gen. xxxii. 12 and elsewhere) with the children of Israel." The surrender, namely, into the hands of the world-power (נָתַן, as in 1 Kings xiv. 16) will continue until the time when one that travails, namely, the mother of the Messiah, seen by God (יוֹלֵדָה, as nameless as Isaiah's הָעַלְמָה), shall have brought forth. First with his birth comes the redemption, the return of the exiles of both kingdoms, the time of judgment of the survivors of his brother, that is, of the Judaean countrymen of the king (יֶתֶר, as Zeph. ii. 9; cf. שְׁאֵרִית, ii. 12), and of those belonging to them from the brother kingdom of Israel. Isaiah also prophesies in chap. xi., in connection with the parousia of the Messiah, the bringing back of the exiles, and the restoration of the unity of the people; but here in Micah the connection is more closely determined.

The prophet then says what the king out of Bethlehem will do, and he who has a nameless one as mother, and of whose father there is no mention (vers. 3–5): "And he shall approach and feed in the power of Yahweh, in the exaltation of the name of Yahweh, and they shall remain dwelling [in possession of their dwelling-places], for from henceforth he stands as a great one there, even unto the ends of the earth [from henceforth, since he has taken the shepherd's staff, that is, the royal sceptre, all the world, willingly or unwillingly, shall bow before his greatness]. And this one shall be peace (cf. Eph. ii. 14: "this is our peace")—Asshur when it shall press into our land and tread our palaces, we will engage against it seven shepherds and eight princes of men. And they feed the land of Asshur with the sword, and the land of Nimrod at its entrances [which are guarded with fortifications], and he secures deliverance from Asshur, in case it presses in, and in case it treads our boundary."

The seven shepherds and eight princes of men, without our being able to solve this peculiar problem further, are his weapons surrounding him like a corona. The image of the Messiah is kept in a martial form, and the thought that the King Messiah protects His people from all hostile powers, gives it its historical form. Although in Micah iv. 10 Zion and Babylon already appear contrasted as at opposite poles, he nevertheless calls the world-empire, as Isaiah, by the historical name at that time, Asshur (Nimrod's country). But while Isaiah beholds the Messiah together with the Assyrian oppressions, and the beginning of his kingdom with the destruction of Asshur, for the more extended view of Micah the parousia of the Messiah is connected with the bringing again from both exiles, as is also to be seen from ii. 12 f.: "Gather, yea I will gather thee, entirely, Jacob; collect, yea I will collect the remnant of Israel, together I will make them like a flock of lambs in firm custody, a herd in the midst of their fit pasture, they [namely, fold and pasture] shall roar on account of men. The dasher in pieces goes before them, they break through and go away [break] through the gate [of the hostile cities, which they held captive] and go out, and their king goes before them, and Yahweh at their head." All Jacob is the Israel of both kingdoms. The breaker through (הַפֹּרֵץ), their king, is the Messiah, the "One Head" in Hosea ii. 2, in which also likewise, as here in Micah, King and Yahweh stand together. Both these march before the reunited people, Yahweh and His Christ. The blending of both, as is expressed in the Isaianic names of the Messiah, עִמָּנוּאֵל and אֵל גִּבּוֹר, remains unexpressed.

CHAPTER VIII.

PROPHECY FROM THE TIME OF HEZEKIAH UNTIL THE CATASTROPHE.

§ 35. *The Domain of Nahum's and Zephaniah's Vision.*

ALTHOUGH Isaiah and Micah foresaw in Babylon the heiress of the Assyrian world-power, nevertheless they are the prophets of the Assyrian period of judgment. First Nahum and Zephaniah bring the Assyrian period to a conclusion. Nahum, from Assyrian Elkosh,[1] hence one of the Assyrian exiles, prophesies, as is apparent from i. 9b, 14, after the miraculous rescue of Jerusalem, whose destruction was threatened by Assyria (701 B.C.), and before Sennacherib's assassination in the temple of Nisroch (681 B.C.), hence toward the end of the government of this king. He predicts the fall of Nineveh (about 607 B.C.), and beholds in this the fall of the world-empire simply, and afterwards the restoration of the unity and glory of entire Israel.

The contents of the work of Zephaniah, who entered

[1] There was a Syrian poet, Israel of Elkosh, who died 793 (*Zeitschrift der Deutschen Morgenländischen Gesellschaft*, xxxi. 65). The place lies on the east bank of the Tigris north of Mosul. The above reference is incorrect.—C.

upon his ministry after the beginning of the purification of the worship of Josiah, probably after his eighteenth year, is varied. He also predicts the judgment upon Nineveh, the metropolis of the world-empire at that time, but at the same time the judgment upon Judah and the surrounding peoples. He does not yet name the Chaldeans as instruments of punishment; but it is the Chaldean period of judgment which he describes as *dies irae dies illa*. All which the prophet has previously said concerning the night of judgment and the light of salvation, and the transition from night to light, is compressed in his work to a mosaic picture. He, as well as Nahum, makes no mention of the person of the Messiah; but in the prophecy of the triumph of salvation, and the new period which dawns for Israel and the nations of the world, he emulates his predecessors. It is a fearful picture of the condition of morals in Jerusalem which he unrolls, because of which he threatens, and in view of the day of wrath near at hand calls to repentance. But even in the round of judgments upon the peoples (chap. ii.), the promise demands a place which concerns the שְׁאֵרִית, the remnant (Zeph. ii. 7, 9) who are preserved in the midst of judgment. A new Israel goes forth from this melting of the fire of wrath, and at the same time the conversion of the peoples to the God of Israel, who has secured for Himself universal recognition (Zeph. ii. 11): "Terrible is [shows Himself] Yahweh over them [Moab and Benê-Ammon, whom the prophet had just threatened, and from whom his range of view was in general extended to the heathen]; for He has caused all the gods of the earth to disappear [properly, He has made them consumptive], and each shall pray to Him from his place, all the islands of the heathen."

In chap. iii. rebuke and threatening are renewed, but only in order that the intensity of the promise may break through all the more strongly. Penal justice is followed by mercy, for which it prepares the way. When the cup of wrath is drained, love is poured forth. This turning-point is fixed by אָז, iii. 9: "For then [after judgment has been visited on the sinful peoples, and the no less sinful people whose capital is Jerusalem] I will turn to the nations a pure lip [that is, I will grant to those who previously called on the idols, and who spoke as idolaters, a purified, consecrated manner of speech], that they may all call upon the name of Yahweh, since they serve Him with one consent." As רָזָה (*emaciavit*), ii. 11, said concerning the heathen gods, is otherwise an exceptional figure of speech of Zephaniah, so here in iii. 9 (*mutabo populis labium purum*) the future conversion of the heathen is expressed in a significant way which is peculiar to him. On the other hand, the prophecy concerning the return of the diaspora of Israel with the friendly help of the nations is as follows (Zeph. iii. 10): "From beyond the rivers of Ethiopia they bring my worshippers, the daughter [totality] of my dispersed, as my offering," exactly as if the prophet, who is pleased with such mosaic style, had blended in a miniature that which is prophesied in Isa. lxvi. 18–20 with the addition of Isa. xviii. 1.

In the description of Israel who are brought back judicially purified, he emphasizes the humility on account of which the congregation again prospers. Israel is blended together in a עַם עָנִי וָדָל, a spiritually poor people, and brought down from a false height, who can trust and rejoice in the name of Yahweh; for, as ver. 15 calls to this new true Israel, "Yahweh hath removed far away thy judgments, hath cleared away thine enemies—the King of Israel, Yahweh, is in the midst of thee, thou hast further to fear no misfortune." And then he describes (ver. 17) the loving relation of Yahweh to this congregation of the future in bold anthropomorphisms which remind us of the mystic erotic manner of Hosea: "Yahweh thy God is in the midst of thee as a helpful hero, He has blissful joy in thee, shall be dumb in His love [since it is unspeakable], shall rejoice over thee with shouting." Yahweh appears here to have become like a man. Beside the King of Israel presented in such a human way, condescending in such lowliness to men, there is neither room for, nor need of a human king.

§ 36. *Habakkuk's Solution of Faith and Faith's Object.*

Among the Old Testament *loci illustres* regarding faith are two in Isaiah (vii. 9, Luther: *gläubet ihr nicht, so bleibet ihr nicht;* and xxviii. 16, Luther: *wer glaubt, der fleucht nicht*). The latter passage belongs to the three, which in the New Testament are each cited three times: Gen. xv. 6; Isa. xxviii. 16; Hab. ii. 4. Habakkuk is one of the prophets who, as is said in 2 Kings xxi. 10–15, xxiii. 26 f., xxiv. 2–4, announces the judgment as henceforth unavoidable. His lamentation concerning the dominant corruption (Hab. i. 2–4) agrees with the fearful characterization of Manasseh and afterwards of Jehoiakim; and his connection with the Psalms, especially those of Asaph (proved in my Commentary, 1843), is to be explained by 2 Chron. xxix. 30. He prophesies the invasion of the Chaldeans and the afflictions which follow in their train, hence before the battle of Carchemish in the fourth year of Jehoiachin (606 B.C.), which decided the supremacy of the Chaldeans in Anterior Asia.

The fundamental thoughts of this book are as follows:—(1) There are two kingdoms in conflict: the kingdom of this world, whose ruler is the king of Chaldea, and the kingdom of God, whose ruler is God's Anointed; (2) the interference of Yahweh helps God's Anointed to the victory; (3) this completion of the work of God in the course of the world's history, when the time previously determined has come, is longed for by the believers; (4) it is faith which, in this conflict of the world against the kingdom of God, escapes the danger of destruction, and which in the midst of death participates in life. It is a theodicy, whose solution of the riddle of the world's history consists in this, that, although God makes use of the wicked for the punishment of the wicked, nevertheless the evil, which is serviceable to Him, finally falls under His judgments, and the good triumphs. These fundamental thoughts are expressed in the form of a dialogue with God. Upon the prophet's question and complaint concerning the secret sinful action (Hab. i. 2–4), follows the answer of God announcing judgment through the Chaldeans (Hab. i. 5–11); and upon the prophet's question and complaint concerning the cruel dealings of the Chaldeans (Hab. i. 12–17), follows the answer of God, announcing judgment upon the Chaldeans (Hab. ii.). The prophet in suspense waits with inward watchfulness to see what answer he shall receive, and what answer he shall give to His question, why the All Holy One can witness so quietly the proud, godless behaviour of the enemy. The answer begins with the command to write it, and exhibit it, in writing which can be easily read (Hab. ii. 2), and the motive of this command is (ver. 3): "for the beholding [that which is beheld] is kept back until the point of time [future fulfilment], and pants for the end [that is, strives for the expiration of the time determined until the consummation [1]], and shall not deceive; if it delays, wait for it, for it will come, yea, it will come, it will not stay away." The

[1] In my commentary, *Der Prophet Habakkuk, ausgelegt* von Franz Delitzsch, Leipzig 1843, the reasons for the translation: "It discourses of the end" seemed to me to predominate—one can be in doubt, but why then this formal expression? I now prefer *anhelat ad finem*, as I also translate Ps. xii. 6: "I will put him in safety, who pants [yearns] for it."

Septuagint translates: ἐὰν ὑστερήσῃ ὑπόμεινον αὐτὸν, ὅτι ἐρχόμενος ἥξει καὶ οὐ μὴ χρονίσῃ, and therefore refers לֹו and that which follows, not to that which is beheld,—the redemption from the servitude through the world-power,—but to One who is given to be beheld—the Redeemer from the world-power. Here it remains questionable whether the Lord or His Anointed is intended. But the Epistle to the Hebrews, which freely adopts the passage without citing it, and transforms the ἐρχόμενος of the Septuagint, corresponding to the intensive infinitive בֹּא into ὁ ἐρχόμενος, doubtless thinks of Christ appearing as judge in glory.

There begins with ver. 4 that which God gives the prophet to behold, the judgment on the lords of the world: "Behold, puffed up, not upright is his soul in him: and the righteous, through his faith shall he live," or after another mode of accentuation—*Tiphcha* with בֶּאֱמוּנָתוֹ:—"And the righteous through his faith— he shall live." We may accentuate this way or that, the meaning is always, that the righteous in the midst of judgment escapes death and remains preserved by means of his own אֱמוּנָה as righteous, that is, of the confidence which holds fast on God and His word, by means of the confidence which builds firmly on the promise of God in spite of the contradictory present, by means of the faithfulness which hangs fast on him, with one word: of the faith which is called אֱמוּנָה, *firmitas* as *firma fiducia*; faith is therefore indicated as the fundamental characteristic which makes the righteous righteous, and by means of which he shall participate in life.

In Hab. ii. 6 ff. a woe (הוֹי), in five strophes, put in the mouth of the mistreated people, announces to the world-conqueror his fall. The prophet means according to i. 6, the Chaldeans, but as representatives of the tyrannical idolatrous world-power which works in vain against the decree of God, " for [as is said, Hab. ii. 14] the earth shall be full of the knowledge of the glory of Yahweh, as the waters that cover the sea."

There follows in chap. iii. upon the two parts, consisting of a dialogue, a תְּפִלָּה, a psalm written in the sublimest style,—as Judg. v. and Ps. lxviii.,—consisting of petitions and contemplations, which are the lyrical echo of the first and second divine answer. Here the prophet praises the appearing of Yahweh in judicial glory, and remembers also His Anointed, not as a mediator, however, but as an object of the redemption which is to be accomplished in judgment (ver. 13): " Thou wentest forth to the help of Thy people, to the help of Thine Anointed" (Septuagint: τοῦ σῶσαι τὸν χριστόν σου; according to another reading: τοὺς χριστούς σου). It is indeed questionable whether אֶת־מְשִׁיחֶךָ should not rather be translated " with Thine Anointed " (Aquila, Quinta: σὺν χριστῳ σου). Jerome considers this translation Christian, and the other Judaizing. But granted that the Messiah is intended in an eschatological sense, an appeal for the accusative construction can be made with equal propriety to

Zech. ix. 9 (where the Messiah is called נוֹשָׁע: one who has become helpful], as for the prepositional to Ps. cx. 5 (the Almighty at thy right hand). It is really probable that the prophet means by the divinely-anointed One, not the king of his time, but of the final period, for he continues, 13*b*: "Thou breakest in pieces the head of the house of the wicked"—the divinely-anointed One is the antithesis of the world-ruler, Christ and Antichrist are contrasted.

§ 37. *Mediately Messianic Elements in Jeremiah's Announcement, until the carrying away of Jehoiachin.*

Jeremiah, who was called, as he himself relates, in the thirteenth year of Josiah, is a contemporary of Zephaniah and Habakkuk, preceding both these in the time when he was called. The history of his call (Jer. i.) is in all directions a prognostic of his official doing and suffering. His calling is directed rather to tearing down than to building up. In this sad office one suffering after another as a confessor befalls him; but notwithstanding the depth and tenderness of his susceptibility, strong in God, he bids defiance to all attacks. In his first address (Jer. ii.-iii. 5) מֵעַתָּה (Jer. iii. 4) indicates the religious transformation which had already begun after the twelfth year of Josiah (2 Chron. xxxiv. 3); and in the second (Jer. iii. 6–vi.), vi. 20 presupposes the purification of worship which was accomplished in the eighteenth year of Josiah. But the prophet sees behind the glittering restoration the ever dominant corruption of morals, and comforts himself with the hope of a final, true, and general conversion, embracing the Israel of both kingdoms, since he lays in the mouth of those who are converting the prayer of confession, entreating for mercy (Jer. iii. 22 f.), as an answer to the divine call to repentance. It can neither be proved, nor is it conceivable, that Jeremiah could have been opposed to the restoration of the worship of Yahweh and the establishment of the sacrificial service at the temple of Jerusalem, which was designed to prevent idolatrous degeneration; for as even private worship as a matter of necessity creates forms of worship, the divine worship of a congregation cannot exist at all without express forms of worship. But the prophetic calling was not especially directed to teaching and shielding these forms of worship, but to that which was essentially religious, with which they must be filled in order not to sink down to deceitful performances, to dead works. The first discourses of Jeremiah show that the people of his time, who boasted that they had the temple, the central seat of Yahweh, in the midst of them (Jer. vii. 4), were sunken in vices, and were always still idolatrous, were so corrupt beyond improvement, that he was not to pray for them. The reformation of Josiah, whose lever was Deuteronomy, restored the legal worship, but as we also see from Zephaniah, without being able to raise the people, who were deeply corrupted in their morals in all classes, including the priests and prophets. We must take this into account in order to understand that Jeremiah could have no pleasure in the sacrificial service (Jer. vi. 20) which had again come into vogue, and in order not to misunderstand so bold an expression as vii. 22 f., in which his antipathy against the self-deception connected with the *opus operatum* of the burnt-offerings and sacrifices went so far that it seems as if he did not recognise a sacrificial torah resting upon divine revelation. The appearance is emphasized, since he says (viii. 8): "How can you say we are wise, and the torah of Yahweh is with us? Truly, behold the deceptive styles of the scribes[1] is active for deception." This sounds as if directed against priestly writings, which gave self-made laws the colour of divine sanction. But that the bringing of sacrifices in vii. 22 f., viii. 8 is lowered to an arbitrary institution, and even as displeasing to God, is disproved through the fact that even Jeremiah is not able to represent the divine service of the final period without sacrifices (see xxxiii. 18; or if one doubts the genuineness of this passage, see xvii. 26, xxxiii. 10),

[1] Not for the purpose of deception, but to deception, in a deceptive manner, as לַשֶּׁקֶר is also used in iii. 23, xxvii. 15; and עָשָׂה without supplying an object, as a conception limited to itself, 2 Sam. xii. 12; Prov. xiii. 6. Jerome renders it correctly: *vere mendacium operatus est* (or *operatur*) *stilus mendax scribarum*. Jeremiah could not have had Deuteronomy in mind on account of the conformity of his language to this book. Nor can the legislation of the Priests' Code be intended, for could this have secured such an undisputed public acceptance if so great a prophet as Jeremiah had uttered his verdict against it?

—sacrifices, indeed, which would not satisfy the letter of the law, but which are the free symbolical expression of thankful worship.

All prophets represent, in opposition to the religion of the letter of the law, the religion of the freedom of the spirit; but none in such a cutting polemic, however, as Jeremiah. The most holy in the most holy place of the temple is the ark of the covenant, the earthly throne of God in the midst of His people; but Jeremiah, hoping for a future renewal of Israel, which shall be more thorough than the present (Jer. iii. 4), prophesies, at the same time, that there shall be no more an ark of the covenant (ver. 16): "In those days—utterance of Yahweh—they shall no longer say, 'The ark of the covenant of Yahweh'; and no thought shall arise concerning it, and ye shall no more think of it, nor miss it, and it shall not be made again." And why not? Because, as is said in ver. 17, all Jerusalem shall be the throne of Yahweh. The prophet is transported into this Messianic period without his mentioning here the Messiah. But it is of importance for the future fulfilment of Messianic prophecy, that in the threatening of Jechoniah (Jer. xxii. 24 ff.) the dominant line of Solomon is deprived of the throne. For so ver. 30 seems to be intended, since the threatening (ver. 24): "Although Coniah, son of Jehoiakim king of Judah, wore the seal ring on my right hand, nevertheless I would tear him off." Its companion piece is found in a prophecy by Haggai (ii. 23): "I will take thee and put thee on as a seal ring," which pertains to Zerubbabel, to whom, according to Luke iii. 31 (cf. Zech. xii. 12), the line of Nathan belonged.[1]

§ 38. *Immediate Messianic Elements in Jeremiah's Prophecies under Zedekiah until after the Destruction of Jerusalem.*

We meet the first immediate Messianic prophecy in the woe upon the shepherds (Jer. xxiii. 1–8), which, as we may conclude from ver. 3, was after the deportation of King Jehoiachin to Babylon with ten thousand of the kernel of the population. The promise begins with the assurance that God will awaken shepherds, according to His will, for His people brought back from banishment, and then proceeds: "Behold days come—utterance of Yahweh—that I will raise up for David a righteous sprout (צֶמַח צַדִּיק), and he shall rule as a king, and shall deal prudently, and shall exercise justice and righteousness in the land; and this is his name with which they shall name him [יִקְרְאוֹ likewise with the most universal subject, like וַיִּקְרָא (Isa. ix. 5), and with *tiphcha* which excludes the connection, 'with which Yahweh shall call him']: 'Yahweh our righteousness'" (יְהוָֹה צִדְקֵנוּ). This prediction will be considered in con-

[1] See my article, "Die zwiefache Genealogie des Messias," No. xii. der Talmudischen Studien, in the *Lutherische Zeitschrift*, 1860, pp. 460–465, and the admirable explanation by Eusebius of ὡς ἐνομίζετο (Luke iii. 23) in the passage quoted by Credner, *Einleitung*, p. 68.

nection with its repetition in a later address. In the tenth year of Zedekiah, as the Chaldeans again lay before Jerusalem, and Jeremiah was held captive in the guard-house, falls the purchase of a piece of land, executed with ceremony, together with the rich promises, Jer. xxxii., which are continued during this imprisonment in chap. xxxiii. If we leave xxxiii. 17 ff. out of account,—because this passage, which is wanting in the Septuagint, is attacked as too ceremonially legal for Jeremiah,—there remains as the keynote of the consolations of these two addresses, that God will turn the captivity of His people, and will restore to them their land for a free possession and commerce.

In this connection there is repeated here, xxiii. 5 f., but with some changes (xxxiii. 14–16): "Behold, days come—utterances of Yahweh—that I will perform the good word which I have spoken to the house of Israel, and concerning the house of Judah [introductory reference to the promise, xxiii. 5 f.]. In that day and at the same time I will cause to sprout for David a sprout of righteousness (צֶמַח צְדָקָה), and he shall exercise justice and righteousness in the land. In the same days Judah shall be redeemed, and shall inhabit Jerusalem safely; and this is the name with which they shall call it (Jerusalem): 'Yahweh our righteousness.'" From chap. xxiii. many interpreters draw the conclusion, because the promise concerning the awakening of right shepherds (ver. 4) precedes, that the sprout is intended collectively of an aftergrowth of Davidic rulers who are pleasing to God; but here in chap. xxxiii. this view is without support, the promise is with reference to one, and the progress from the צֶמַח of Isa. iv. 2 to the shoot from the stump of Jesse (Isa. xi. 1) makes it unquestionable that the post-Isaianic prophet means that the Messiah is the second David. Also a welcome light falls upon the name of the Messiah, יְהֹוָה צִדְקֵנוּ from the names עִמָּנוּאֵל and אֵל גִּבּוֹר, which the Messiah has in Isaiah. He is so called in Isaiah, because the strong victorious God is in him, represents Himself in him, makes Himself historically present in him to His people; and here in Jeremiah he is called יְהֹוָה צִדְקֵנוּ, because Yahweh, as our righteousness, that is, as the one making righteous, redeeming from the curse and bondage of sin, dwells in him, is called like Jerusalem יְהֹוָה צִדְקֵנוּ, because now Yahweh, as the one making righteous, forgiving sins (Isa. xxxiii. 24), and renewing morally, has his dwelling in her. The Messiah is called thus as the personal, and Jerusalem as the local revelation of the God[1] who

---

[1] The Septuagint translates: καὶ τοῦτο τὸ ὄνομα αὐτοῦ ὃ καλέσει αὐτὸν ὁ κύριος Ἰωσεδέκ, that is, יְהוֹצָדָק (see Workman, *The Text of Jeremiah*, Edinburgh 1889, p. 239). The translation is absurd; for we do not expect a real historical *nomen proprium*, but an emblematical name. In the proper name Jehozadak: "Yahweh has or retains justice," the expression is the acknowledgment, mark, motto of the one that is to be named, and mediately of the one who is named; on the contrary, יְהֹוָה צִדְקֵנוּ (whether we translate it "Yahweh is our righteousness," or "Yahweh is our God"), as the name of the Messiah and as the name of Jerusalem demands, an actual characteristic relation to that which the name expresses.

transforms the unrighteous desiring righteousness into the righteous.

A year later, on the second of Tammuz of the eleventh year of Zedekiah, after a siege of eighteen months, Jerusalem became a prey of the invading Chaldeans. Jeremiah was compelled, in the midst of the other exiles, and, like them, to wander in fetters to Rama; but there, on account of a command of Nebuchadnezzar which had reached him, his fortune changed—the decision was left to him, he preferred to remain in the land, and went to Gedaliah, to the son of his friend, and the one who had rescued his life, Ahikam (Jer. xxvi. 24), as is related in chap. xxxix. more briefly, and in chap. xl. more extensively.

In chap. xl. 1 a word of Yahweh received by Jeremiah, at that time in Rama, is introduced, but none follows. It is certain that this word of Yahweh is none other than the one introduced in xxx., xxxi. with the same formula, consisting in comforting predictions, written down by the prophet at the special command of God, among which the lamentation of Rachel in Ramah because of the departure of her children, and with reference to their future return, indicates the place where they were received.

Beginning with כֹּה אָמַר יְהוָה, one comforting picture follows another. We emphasize particularly, out of this floral chain of promises, those of a Messianic, and expressly of a New Testament, character.

1. The promise is made to the people (Jer. xxx. 21; cf. xxxiii. 20–22), that in the future they shall

have glorious princes, who are privileged to exercise priestly functions, who are all overtopped by the one second David (Jer. xxx. 9): "And they shall serve Yahweh their God, and David their king, whom I will awake for them." It is certainly questionable whether also in ver. 21 the singular form of the word does not refer to a second David: "And their prince shall come from themselves [from the restored people], and their ruler shall go forth from the midst of them [this people, since foreign dominion has an end]; and I will cause him to approach me, and to draw near to me [so near, namely, as was previously permitted only to the priests]: for who might otherwise dare to draw near to me? Utterance of Yahweh." We see from this, which is also significant for Pentateuch criticism, that Jeremiah recognises the exclusive right of the priests to the arrangements of the divine service in the inner department of the sanctuary, but that he promises to the Israelitish kings of the period of consummation a participation in the priestly prerogatives. Since, however, this stands on a lower plain than the later prophecy, that the future Zemach shall be king and priest in one person, probably in the view of the prophet אַדִּיר as well as נָשִׂיא in the new legislation of Ezekiel is to be distinguished from the other David (דָּוִד מַלְכָּם, 9b), and the expression is not meant exclusively of one.[1]

2. An allegorical reference to the birth of the

[1] Cf. Baudissin, *Die Geschichte des Alttestamentlichen Priesterthums*, Leipzig 1889, p. 246.

Messiah appears to be contained in xxxi. 22: "How long wilt thou go hither and thither, thou backsliding daughter? For Yahweh hath created a new thing in the land: the woman shall shield the man." By means of כִּי the reason is given for the interrogative "how long," from an impulse given by God through a new creation to conversion. The new creation, as is shown in the choice of the sexual expressions נְקֵבָה and גֶּבֶר, consists in a transformation of the relation, which was otherwise according to nature, of both sexes to each other. With von Orelli we understand סוֹבֵב according to Deut. xxxii. 10, Ps. xxxii. 10, but not so that נְקֵבָה indicates the naturally weak, helpless congregation, to which the people is indebted for its protection and preservation;[1] but so that נְקֵבָה, like the עַלְמָה of Isaiah and the יֹלֵדָה of Micah, indicates the mother of the Messiah: A woman shall be a protection, a wall, a fortress of men, since she shall bear the defender of Israel. Thus we understand the causal כִּי better. In Micah v. 2 the birth of the one who bears is considered the turning-point for the conversion of Israel from the labyrinth of the exile.

3. Jeremiah is the prophet who combines the future renewal of the covenant in the conception, and

[1] If נְקֵבָה were to be referred to the congregation, it would be preferable to explain: The woman shall go around the man; that is, the congregation to whom Yahweh is married, and who have become untrue to Him, shall surround Him, seeking to win His love,—the כִּי which gives the reason is adapted to this explanation. But for what purpose is the investiture of this hope (cf. Hos. ii. 9) in such an enigmatical paradox?

the word בְּרִית חֲדָשָׁה (Jer. xxxi. 31–34, cf. the Septuagint, Heb. viii. 8, διαθήκη καινή): "Behold days come—utterance of Yahweh—that I will make with the house of Israel and with the house of Judah a new covenant; not like the covenant which I made with their fathers, in the day that I took them by the hand, to lead them out of the land of Egypt; which covenant of mine they have broken, so that I was displeased against them [בָּחַלְתִּי=בָּעַלְתִּי, Zech. xi. 8, if גָּעַלְתִּי should not be read as in xiv. 19, Septuagint; Heb. viii. 9, κἀγὼ ἠμέλησα αὐτῶν] — utterance of Yahweh. For this is the covenant which I will make with the house of Israel after those days—utterance of Yahweh: I will give my torah within them, and upon their hearts I will write it; and I will be their God, and they shall be my people. And they shall not teach any more one his neighbour, and one his brother, saying: Know Yahweh! For all together they shall know me, from the least among them even to the greatest: for I will forgive their guilt, and I will no more remember their sins." The new covenant is one held in equal honour with the Sinaitic, and which stands on the same plane with it. It is not to be a legal covenant, whose promises are conditioned through the consideration of rules established by documents. The foundation of this new covenant will be the forgiveness of sin as the foundation of the beginning of a new life. In place of the external letters of the law will be those written in the heart, from which the will of God shall determine the conduct; and

MESSIANIC ELEMENTS IN JEREMIAH.

while heretofore the deeper living knowledge was the possession of a few, especially of the prophets, it will then be a common possession, since as Jeremiah had immediately said before (xxxi. 28 f.), personality shall be established in its rights, and shall be removed beyond the consequences of family connection, in which hitherto it had been bound,—a theme which Ezekiel, proceeding from the same popular proverb (chap. xviii.), discusses more fully. The style of these comforting addresses (Jer. xxx., xxxi.) is in part quite Deutero-Isaianic. We see in xxx. 8–10 the beginning of the representation of Israel as עֶבֶד יְהוָה: "And it shall come to pass in that day—utterance of Yahweh of hosts: I will break his yoke from off thy neck, and will tear his bands in pieces, and it [my people] shall not again be slaves (יַעַבְדוּ) to strangers. And they shall serve (וְעָבְדוּ) Yahweh their God, and I will awake for them David their king. And thou, fear not, my servant Jacob (עַבְדִּי יַעֲקֹב)." Here, remarks Hitzig, עַבְדִּי is introduced through וְעָבְדוּ. Further on in the appendix to the prophecy against Egypt (Jer. xlvi. 27 f.), which is partially Deutero-Isaianic (cf. Isa. xliii. 1–6), but has partially the characteristics of Jeremiah, עֶבֶד יַעֲקֹב occurs without any such introduction, just as in Isa. xli. 8, as a complete idea.

CHAPTER IX.

PROPHECY IN THE BABYLONIAN EXILE.

§ 39. *The Messiah in Ezekiel.*

IN the midst of Jeremiah's activity occurred the deportation of Jehoiachin which followed the battle at Carchemish (606 B.C.). Among the ten thousand who shared the fate of the king was also Ezekiel, son of Buzi the priest, who, after he had settled in Tel-Abib, on the Babylonian Chaboras, in the fifth year of the deportation, was called as prophet. When he became prophet, he was not false to the priesthood, whose calling had to do with the handling of the legal torah. In this respect he stands in sharp contrast with Jeremiah, who, although he was also a כֹּהֵן (priest), yet had no warm interest in the ceremonial law. There is no book of any other prophet which is so pictorial as that of Ezekiel. Heavenly and earthly things transform themselves for him into plastic pictures, which he describes even to the minutest details, with which this is connected, that the co-operation of the fancy and of the understanding in the act of prophesying is especially influential with him. The manner of his call is at once characteristic.

The fact that it is God who rules the world in judicial omnipotence, that names Ezekiel as the prophet of the judgment upon Jerusalem, is established by a vision of unparalleled grandeur. While Isaiah, caught up to heaven, is called by the One enthroned there, who is surrounded by the seraphim, in Ezekiel it is the One inhabiting the universe, riding upon the chariot, the royal waggon borne by the cherubim and *ofannim*, who sweeps down to the one who is to be called. And while in Isaiah the One enthroned is indeed visible, but covered by a long garment, in Ezekiel the heavenly charioteer appears in unveiled human form, which shines from the loins and upwards like *chasmal* (amber), and downwards like fire. John the evangelist is so bold as to say that Isaiah beheld the doxa of the future Christ (xii. 41). If, as is presupposed in this passage, Yahweh, who granted that His prophet should behold Him in human form, is identical with the human [elements] which appeared in Christ, the Johannean εἶδε τὴν δόξαν αὐτοῦ is still more true of Ezekiel than of Isaiah, for the One who is enthroned permits himself to be seen as a real man (כְּמַרְאֵה אָדָם, Ezek. i. 26). But these are lights which fall only upon those preprophetic visions for him who has recognised the incarnation as the end of the ways of God. We turn to another significant picture composed by Ezekiel, which is properly Messianic, and does not first appear from a Christian standpoint in a Christological light. We mean the prophecy concerning the grape vine and the sprout of the cedar in chap. xvii., which, in so far as it has an apocalyptic character, is received into the composition of the picture of the future as already past events—the removal of Jehoiachin and the appointment of Mattaniah-Zedekiah, perhaps also Zedekiah's connection with Egypt. The opening of this view into the future falls, according to viii. 1 (according to the date of the second book, viii.–xix.), in the sixth year of the deportation, hence in the second year of the activity of the prophet. The grape vine, which, planted by the Babylonian eagle, perishes because of its treacherous inclination to the Egyptian eagle, is Zedekiah, and the tender sprout of the Davidic cedar, which, planted by Yahweh on Zion, grows to a cedar overtopping and overshadowing the nations, is the Messiah. The unnoticeable, humble beginning of the Messianic kingdom, which is indicated in the רַךְ of xvii. 22b reminds us in fact and in form of Isa. xi. 1, liii. 2; and the growth of the tender sprout to a glorious cedar, ver. 23, is re-echoed in the parable of the Lord concerning the grain of mustard seed (Matt. xiii. 31 f.); also the word of the Lord (Matt. xxiii. 12): "He who exalteth himself shall be abased," etc., refers to Ezek. xvii. 24 as the moral of the allegory.

This principle of the moral world also finds expression in the threatening prediction against Zedekiah in chap. xxi., according to the date of the third book (xx.–xxiii.), from the seventh year after the deportation, and hence only a few years before the fall of

Jerusalem. In xxi. 23-27 the prophet describes how the king of Babylon stands at the parting of two ways, one of which leads to Rabbath Ammon, the other to Jerusalem, the treacherous (cf. xvii. 5) and yet secure city, as it thinks, on account of its oath of vassalage. "And thou"—with these words, xx. 30-32, the prophet turns himself to Zedekiah—" pierced through [fulfilled through the putting out of his eyes, Jer. xxxix. 7], blasphemer, prince of Israel, whose day has come at the time of the guilt of the end [that is, which demands the final judgment]; thus saith the Almighty, Yahweh: The mitre shall be removed [הַמִּצְנֶפֶת, the head-band which designated the high priest], and the crown shall be taken away [הָעֲטָרָה, the designation of honour of the king]; it shall not remain: the lowly shall be exalted, and the high shall be brought low (cf. xvii. 24). Overthrow, overthrow, overthrow I bring upon them [upon mitre and crown, high priesthood and kingdom]; also they [this twofold dignity in its degenerate representatives] shall be destroyed [לֹא הָיָה like Isa. xv. 6; Job vi. 21], until he comes to whom the government [הַמִּשְׁפָּט, as in Hos. v. 1] belongs, and I give it to him." Whether that which precedes these closing words is interpreted as we or as others interpret it, it is more than probable that the prophet, by עַד־בֹּא אֲשֶׁר לוֹ הַמִּשְׁפָּט וּנְתַתִּיו, alludes to עַד כִּי יָבֹא שִׁלֹה (Gen. xlix. 10), since he explains it in entirely the same way as Onkelos and the second Jerusalem Targum, עַד דְּיֵיתֵי מְשִׁיחָא דְדִילֵהּ הִיא מַלְכוּתָא. We are not thereby compelled to regard this as the original meaning of שלה (Shiloh); but there are three conclusions we can draw from this old interpretation of Ezekiel of this word in Jacob's blessing of Judah: (1) that the prophet regards it as a Messianic prophecy; (2) that he did not have שילה according to the Massoretic writing, but שלה without yodh in his text; and (3) that, even at a very ancient period, שלה was understood in the sense of שֶׁלֹּה, equivalent to שֶׁלּוֹ, *is cujus est* (*scil. regnum*), as a designation of the Messiah.

In the predictions against the nations (xxv.–xxxii.), which can be inserted between the beginning and end of the fourth book (xxiv., xxxiii. 1–20) as a fifth, a promise which may be compared with Isa. xix. 23 ff. is wanting; but this deficit is covered through the conclusion of chap. xvi. — the terrible picture of the moral condition of Jerusalem in comparison with that of her sisters, Sodom and Gomorrah. This conclusion agrees essentially with the conclusion of Paul's outline of the history of redemption (Rom. xi. 32 ff.): the end of human history is this, that the compassion of God, surpassing the greatness of the sin, raises all, Sodom, Samaria, and even Judah, from the pit—a time of universal grace which rescues all that is to be rescued, even that which has fallen into Hades. While Jerusalem lies in the death struggle, dumbness is inflicted upon Ezekiel (xxiv. 25 ff.).

The discourses of the sixth book (xxxiii. 21–xxxix.) begin, as the later information reaches the prophet at Tel-Abib, that the sufferings of Jerusalem have ended, and now the string of his tongue is loosed. The second of these addresses (Ezek. xxxiv.) is directed against the self-seeking, unscrupulous shepherds: Yahweh Himself will take His own herd (xxxiv. 23 f.): "And I will appoint over them a shepherd (רֹעֶה אֶחָד), and he shall feed them; my servant David, he shall feed them, and he shall be their shepherd. I, Yahweh, will be their God, and my servant David prince (נָשִׂיא) in their midst: I, Yahweh, have spoken it." This promise is repeated (xxxvii. 23b, 24): "I will purify them, and they shall be my people, and I will be their God. And my servant David is king (מֶלֶךְ) over them, and they all [Israel of both kingdoms] have one shepherd, and they shall walk in my laws, and my statutes shall they observe and execute."

Hitzig thinks that Ezekiel has the awakening of David from the dead in prospect; but the meaning of the promise is nothing else than Hos. iii. 5; Jer. xxx. 9. A king is intended who is David's antitype, and this king is not one who, like others, transmits his throne, for God gives His people in him רֹעֶה אֶחָד, one instead of many, and hence probably one for ever.

§ 40. *The Prince in Ezekiel's Future State.*

One for ever? The case would be different if the prince (נָשִׂיא), whom Ezekiel embodies with his ecclesiastical and political ideal of the future, were to be identified with the "King David" of the promise; for this prince has children and successors—he is nothing less than an absolute personality. This torah of the future does not recognise a high priest. But this prince, far from taking the place of the pontifex, is rather a layman. His relation to the priesthood and sanctuary is sharply defined; his chief pre-eminence consists only in his being able to hold sacrificial meals in the hall of the east door,—the east door itself, through which the doxa of Yahweh entered the temple, remains closed. The sacrificial duties of the prince are exactly indicated, and such dynastic excesses as have occurred before are prevented through exact regulations regarding the prince's possession. The son of the prince, who is designated as his successor, is also universal heir. The domain is so great that the prince can also remember his other sons with gifts, but he is not allowed to give to others besides his own lawful heirs of his landed property. Even such presents as he makes to his servants return in the year of jubilee to the Crown. Only those are persuaded that this prince is the Messiah who begin with the πρῶτον ψεῦδος that the future temple of Ezekiel is an allegory of the New Testament Church. This prince has nothing whatever in common with the Messiah; it is not demanded or expressly presupposed that he belongs to the house of David. If he were the Messiah, then there would be no Messiah at all—that is, no final ideal king of absolute significance, and with a calling reaching beyond the national limitations to mankind. But he recognises indeed the lofty form of the second David, also his last prophetic word (Ezek. xxix. 21), from the twenty-seventh year of the deportation, the sixteenth after the destruction of Jerusalem: " On that day I will cause a horn to bud for the house of Israel" —probably has in view the King Messiah (Ps. cxxxii. 17, cf. Luke i. 69). How does it come about now that, in the outline of the existence of the congregation of Israel in the final period, which is clothed in vision, that noble form has disappeared from his horizon? It has come about because the Messiah is more than a temporal reigning prince, because the princely dignity in the future State is too small for Him. It is significant that the prophet, while he sketches the picture of the future State, leaves the Messiah out of account. When the Jewish people again becomes an independent State, as is expected by all the prophets, it must also have a king, must have princes. But that the Messiah shall be this king is not only an impossible representation for the New Testament consciousness, but also, as here appears in Ezekiel, for the Old Testament. For this reason there is in the prophetic view of the future an unremoved antinomy which is most striking in Ezekiel, because he paints everything to the smallest details. For also in Isaiah (vii.-xi.) the question is raised, Is the second David a king who first arises, and dies and makes room for another? We must answer this question in the negative; and if, therefore, a Jewish State in the future should have a king who traced his ancestry back to David, he would not be the Messiah, he has more divine than earthly greatness, he is a personality of religious, and not merely of political significance. The exaltation of his person and of his calling resists his introduction into an ideal State which is purely natural, although it may belong to the final period, like Ezekiel's republic. There is in no prophet anything which can be compared with these chapters (Ezek. xl.–xlviii.). Ezekiel is the only prophet who knows that he is not only called by God to be prophet, but also at the same time as reformer. We must know the history of worship, and the history of the state of the Jewish people more exactly, in order everywhere to discern against what evil conditions which had found place his reform was directed. At times he says himself expressly, as in chap. xliv., when he limits the service of the sanctuary to the priests of Zadok, and the Levites who are subordinated to them, with the exclusion of uncircumcised Israelites, and (xlv. 8) after the unchangeable measurement of the land of the prince, he continues: "My princes shall no longer oppress the people." Whether the new legislation is intended for the time of the return from the exile, or for the final period, we should not ask at all.

As the development of the last things was contemporaneous for the primitive Church with the destruction of Jerusalem on account of the peculiar eschatological addresses of the Lord, so the final period is joined for all prophets with the gathering of Israel from all lands among which they had been scattered. In chap. xxxvii. Ezekiel prophesies the bringing again from the exile under the image of a resurrection; and in chaps. xxxviii., xxxix., the last attack of the heathen world, under the leadership of Gog from the land of Magog, against the entire house of Israel, which has returned to its native land. The new torah is designed for this Israel at the end of the exile. Without denying the authority of the old legislation for the present,—which, as Ezekiel wrote, had certainly been codified in the Jehovistic book of history and of law, if not in the Priests' Code, — he promulgated a new code, in case that the Israel of both kingdoms, ashamed of its former offences (Ezek. xliii. 10 f.), should return from banishment. In the year 536 B.C. and afterwards, only a small portion of the people had returned, who rightly did not regard the torah of Ezekiel as having binding force, since the realization of its conditions were wanting, and this realization, notwithstanding all deviations, was preceded by the foundation of the new covenant upon the basis of the torah which was built upon the Sinaitic legal covenant, which excludes every repristination of the shadow of works; for Christ is the end of the law. But, nevertheless, no interpreter can say how much of the ideal of Ezekiel will be realized when the καιροὶ ἐθνῶν (Luke xxi. 24) are passed, and Israel shall be restored to his new land, full of blessing and prosperity.

§ 41. *The Metamorphosis of the Messianic Ideal in Isa.* xl.–lxvi.

We now turn from Ezekiel, the prophetic reformer of the character of the congregation, to the author of the thrice nine addresses on the exiles (Isa. xl.–xlviii., xlix.–lvii., lviii.–lxvi.), who has a higher significance as reformer, since he is the reformer of the Messianic ideal. If Isaiah, who was called in the year of Uzziah's death, were the author of these addresses, the Babylonian exile would not be his actual, but his ideal present. In fact, there are weighty grounds for Isaiah's authorship, which at least two of the later [critics], Klostermann and Bredenkamp, have allowed to influence them; the former helping himself through the supposition that an heir of the Isaianic spirit freely reproduced posthumous prophecies of the master, which had to do with the Babylonian exile;[1] the latter believing that from the time of that exile the proto-Isaianic elements, which belong at the beginning of the web of these Deutero-Isaianic prophecies, may be still recognised here and there. Leaving these hypotheses aside, we hold that without a doubt Isaiah participated essentially in this book of consolation for the exiles. The author, although not an immediate pupil of Isaiah, is yet a prophet of his school: he is by birth equal with the master in spirit and gifts. Not without the influence of an advance and change in the age, he even surpasses him, and shows his reciprocal relation to the Book of Jeremiah, since in many places he reproduces Jeremianic thoughts with bold independence in a higher tone, and with an Isaianic stamp. In many respects we might sooner hold that Jeremiah

---

[1] *Zeitschrift für die gesammte lutherische Theologie und Kirche,* Leipzig 1876, pp. 1–60.

is the one who reproduced [the passage in question]; but the weighty grounds for Isaiah's priority are cast aside by two preponderating reasons: (1) that if we hold that Isaiah is the author of xl.–lxvi. we must maintain a phenomenon which otherwise is without a parallel in the prophetic literature, for otherwise it is everywhere peculiar to prophecy that it goes out from the present, and does not transport itself to the future, without returning to the ground of its own contemporary history; but Isaiah would live and act here in the exile, and address the exiles through twenty-seven chapters, without coming back from his ideal to his actual present. (2) The pedagogical progress in the recognition and progress of salvation, divinely ordered, demands the origin of these addresses under the impulses given by the exile. Zephaniah, Habakkuk, Jeremiah, and Ezekiel would represent an incomprehensible retrogression if the author of Isa. xl.–lxvi. were not younger than Jeremiah, younger even than Ezekiel, and did not have the last third of the exile as his historical station. It is indeed all the more incomprehensible that this great prophet should have become an anonymous for the congregation who returned to the Holy Land, of whom he was a contemporary, and that his forgotten name was covered with that of Isaiah; but we must accept these and other incomprehensible things in order to escape that which was most incomprehensible of all, that it is one and the same prophet to whom we are indebted for the image of the second David in Isa. vii.–xi., and the image of the servant of Yahweh in xl.–lvi. Isaiah, who was called in the year of the death of Uzziah, although he was not the creator, was nevertheless the developer of the idea of the Messiah; the image of King Messiah, previously only a shadowy outline, becomes in chaps. vii.–xi. a picture in rich colours with three panels. In chaps. xl.–lxvi., on the contrary, nothing is said concerning a Messiah a son of David. It is the people to whom Yahweh offers an everlasting covenant, since He actualizes the inviolable promises which were made to David. Only Yahweh is called everywhere King of Israel (xliv. 6, xliii. 15). The idea of King Messiah disappears in the idea of the Messianic people. Israel is designed to be, as the introduction to the Sinaitic legislation says, a מַמְלֶכֶת כֹּהֲנִים (Ex. xix. 6). Deutero-Isaiah reaches back to this idea of Israel as the people of mediation. Certainly this is connected with the loss which the Davidic kingdom suffered after Zedekiah. Jeremiah and Ezekiel, who experienced the catastrophe either wholly or partially, and had a fresh recollection of it, vie with each other in promises of another David; but it was given to the second Isaiah, who was born in the exile, to look through the redemptive historical mission of Israel, from the removal of his people into the heathen world in new great connections, from which he receives back the idea of the Messiah transfigured and enriched, and so to lead the Messianic proclamation into a new path, within which it moves among the post-exilic prophets, including David. The *ecce-homo*-characteristic and the work of the Messiah are hereafter received into the image of the Messiah. The idea of the servant of Yahweh is bridge and ladder to these new means of knowledge.

§ 42. *The Servant of Yahweh in Deutero-Isaiah.*

Israel is the servant of Yahweh — Israel as the people whom the call of Abraham had in view, as the people called to the service of Yahweh, and for the advancement of the work which has for its object the salvation of the human race (xli. 8). But the mass is unequal to this ideal of a people serving the highest ends of God; it is untrue towards Yahweh, and incapable of Israel's mediating mission, blind with seeing eyes, and deaf with hearing ears (xliii. 8), so that the prophet has to complain (xlii. 19): "Who is blind, if not my servant, and deaf as my messenger, whom I send?" Nevertheless there are such who not only belong externally to the people of redemptive history, but also really serve the God of salvation in reverence and confession, in spite of the hostility which meets them. Such significant words as xliv. 2 refer to them: "Fear not, my servant Jacob, and Jeshurun, whom I have chosen." Their spiritual character is indicated (li. 7): "Hearken to me, who know righteousness, oh people, in whose heart is my law." But in this inner circle the conception of the עֶבֶד יְהוָה does not remain; it is still further contracted to an individual centre, to one who is called יִשְׂרָאֵל (xlix. 3), because he is Israel in highest potency, the perfect reality of that which Israel is to be, and the transcendent realization of that which he is to accomplish. The calling of this servant of God, in which the idea of Israel as the servant of God culminates, is addressed first to his own people (xlii. 6, xlix. 8): "I make thee for a covenant of the people, for a light of the heathen;" it is therefore not a collective identical with the mass of the people, with the kernel of the people. The description of him and his utterances is so individual that the personification of a plurality is excluded. We are prevented from thinking of the prophet, the author of these addresses, because this servant of Yahweh (xlii. 1) is introduced by God Himself, and is passed before us in an objective way: "Behold, my servant, whom I have chosen, my elect, with whom my soul is pleased—I have put my Spirit upon him." The prophet hears this ἐν πνεύματι: that which is described is an ideal form of the future. Now, when this second, this Babylonian Isaiah appears, Cyrus has already begun his victorious course; his casting down of idolatrous peoples makes way for the work of the servant of Yahweh, whose victorious power is the word of the Spirit. His entrance upon his ministry belongs to the חֲדָשׁוֹת, which Yahweh announces through the prophets (xlii. 9). The transition to this view of the servant of Yahweh as present is formed by xlviii. 16, where the future One, as with a sudden ἰδοὺ ἥκω, breaks through the secret of his parousia and appears upon the theatre of the present: "And now the Almighty Yahweh hath sent me and His Spirit." From chap. xlviii. 16 the prophet not only hears words of God from and to His servant, but the servant himself takes up the word, xlix. 1 ff. He it is in whom Yahweh came to His people without finding a hearing (l. 2); and he, His servant, also himself complains (l. 4–9) that he came to his own, and his own received him not. It is only questionable who is the one in lxi. 1 ff.—whether the servant of Yahweh or the prophet—who rejoices over his calling to preach the gospel as especially glorious. The decision is here and elsewhere difficult, because that the address of the servant of Yahweh loses itself unobserved in the address of Yahweh or in the address of the prophet, but yet only in the objective address of the prophet, whose "I" only once evidently appears in the refrain of the second paragraph (lvii. 21). In every place where the servant of Yahweh appears speaking in immediate self-representation in the field of vision of the prophet, the appearance of the future One is not long maintained on this its greatest height—even in lxi. 4–9 prophecy and the address of Yahweh are introduced in the midst of the address of the one who is rejoicing there.

§ 43. *The Mediator of Salvation as Prophet, Priest, and King in one Person.*

All forms of the previous representation of redemption removed from their isolation are united in the person of the עֶבֶד יְהוָה (servant of Yahweh), the prophet like Moses, the King Messiah, the priest after the order of Melchizedek. Isaiah demands (xii. 4) the preaching of the great deeds of Yahweh in the world of nations. In Deutero-Isaiah we see the execution of this demand brought about through the servant of Yahweh, who does not rest nor repose until he has secured the recognition of the religion of the God of revelation in the heathen world. The servant of Yahweh is therefore a prophet, and more than Jonah, whose unique mission only belongs to the shadow, which the one who is in the process of coming casts before himself; his apostleship comprises the entire race. He is also a king who, removed from his humiliation, shall shine in a so transcendent royal glory, that the kings of the earth shall cast themselves at his feet in mute astonishment (xlix. 7, lii. 15).

He is also a priest; he exercises a priestly expiation after he has offered his own life as אָשָׁם, that is, as a propitiatory sacrifice, which atones and makes amends for the sins of his people. Thus we read in the great prophecy of the passion (lii. 13–liii.), which makes such an impression of a definite person, and not of a personified plurality, that Ewald and others think that the prophet has here embodied an ancient martyr-picture into the connection of his address concerning the doings and sufferings of the true Israel. But the servant of Yahweh suffers, indeed freely, not only as a noble man can take all kinds of sufferings upon himself, in order to ward them off from others, or also that in this way, through the transference of sufferings, welfare may arise for others; but the servant of Yahweh, the guiltless one, loads himself with the guilt of his people in order to make it possible for God without injury to His holiness to suffer grace instead of justice to visit the sinner. Since as an antitype of the sacrificial animal he takes upon himself the sins of his people, he thus executes God's decree; it pleased God to crush him, He purposely allowed him to sink in the deepest woe (liii. 10), for his purpose was directed to the fruit of his suffering; He permitted the guilt of us all to storm upon him, and hence His wrath to go over him, in order to make in him, His beloved, a justified and sanctified congregation of His people. No man, according to Ps. xlix. 8 f., can give for another a כֹּפֶר (ransom) in order to release him from death; in case a man like Moses (Ex. xxxii. 32) or Paul (Rom. ix. 3) should offer himself as willing to suffer vicariously the death deserved by the sinner, God would not accept this offer,—only the absolutely guiltless holy servant of God is capable of bringing an offering which covers sin and breaks its power, since in the offering of himself God's own decree of love is executed as a morally effective deed of love. If we consider who speaks of himself in chap. liii. as "we" and "us," this also decides that the servant of Yahweh cannot be the congregation of confessors and martyrs in the exile. It is indeed the Israel of the final period, who in chap. liii. penitently confesses its sin against the servant of God; and this servant, whose innocent shed blood rested hitherto as a national guilt upon the one making confession, is to be considered a collective? But even the one who is unwilling to recognise the Lamb of God, who bears the sins of the world, in this chapter written as it were under the cross upon Golgotha, even such an one must admit that the Deutero-Isaianic prophecy concerning the servant of God is the workshop in which the New Testament ideal of the Messiah comes to realization—the model for a new, more spiritual image of the Messiah, which unites all inalienable elements of the former in itself. In the mirror of this prophecy the Messiah beheld Himself. It became His guiding star upon the way of His calling, and He became its fulfilment.

§ 44. *The Great Finale, Isa.* xxiv.–xxvii.

The Deutero - Isaianic prediction concerning the servant of Yahweh appears to be the *ne plus ultra* of New Testament knowledge in the Old Testament; but in many respects it is surpassed through the cycle of prophecies, Isa. xxiv.–xxvii., which, according to the present arrangement of the Book of Isaiah, form the finale to the oracles concerning the nations (xiii.–xxiii.). This finale is one of the greatest achievements of Old Testament prophecy. The language, accumulating paronomasia on paronomasia, is here address and music at the same time, and the form which the prophecy takes is at the same time epic and lyric; the prophet prophesies mostly in songs taken from the heart of the redeemed congregation. And this imitative musical sound, this hymnological character, is only the incomparable form of an incomparable train of thought. We place this finale after Deutero-Isaiah, because the state of knowledge which is represented therein goes far beyond the Assyrian Isaiah, far beyond Jeremiah and Ezekiel, partially also beyond II. Isaiah. When the prophet (xxvii. 12 f.) represents the diaspora of Israel as returning from Egypt, there seems to be mirrored in it the form of the time of Isaiah, in which Egypt and Asshur were the two great powers (xi. 11). But what is then the קִרְיַת תֹּהוּ (xxiv. 10, cf. xxv. 2, xxvi. 5 f.), whose fall is the middle point of the judgment against the world which is hostile to God, and the turning-point in the redemption of Israel and of the nations? It appears to be Babylon, but it is not the Babylon which was conquered by Cyrus. All which apparently pertains to the history of the times in these chapters xxiv.–xxvii. is emblematical, and merely supplies the colours to the eschatological pictures. The catastrophe of the metropolis of the world appears in connection with the judgment and destruction of the world, and with the destruction of the world (xxiv. 19 f.), and with the judgment of the world the prophet beholds the judgment upon the demoniacal powers which are active in the world's history (xxiv. 21-23). The redemption of Israel does not merely consist in an outward restoration, but in an internal renewal (xxvi. 1–4). And the conversion of the heathen is symbolized as a participation in a feast (xxv. 6): "And Yahweh the Lord prepares for all peoples upon this mountain (that is, Zion as the centre of God's redemption) a feast of fat food, a feast of wine on the lees (that is, which has lain a long while and is thoroughly fermented), of fat food, rich in marrow, of wine on the lees thoroughly strained," and as an unveiling (xxv. 7): "And He removes upon this mountain [that is, Zion as the central place of the accomplishment] the veil which veiled all peoples, and the covering which rested on all nations." But still more than this. In the new Jerusalem Deutero-Isaiah compares the duration of the life of man with the high age which a tree reaches. He who dies when he is a hundred years old will be considered as dying in his youth (lxv. 20–22). In spite, therefore, of the long duration of life, death still reigns; but the author of the finale prophesies (xxv. 8): "He swallows up (בִּלַּע, of absorption, equivalent to annihilation) death for ever, and the Almighty Yahweh wipes the tears from every face, and the disgrace of His people he removes from the entire earth: for Yahweh hath spoken it." And yet more than that. While the oppressors of Israel must be destroyed, without rising to life, the field of corpses of the people of God will become through heavenly dew a resurrection field: the congregation of those who survive the time of judgment will be supplemented through those who are raised from the dead (xxvi. 14–19):

"My dead shall live again, my corpses shall arise; wake up and rejoice, ye who lie in the dust! For the dew of the heavenly bodies is thy dew, and the earth shall bring forth shades." It is the entire New Testament Apocalypse which we have here before us *in nuce*, only that, as also in 1 Cor. xv., the discourse is exclusively concerning the resurrection to life, and is also limited to the narrow frame of the $\pi\rho\omega\tau\eta$ $\dot{a}\nu\dot{a}\sigma\tau a\sigma\iota\varsigma$ (Rev. xx. 5 f.). In general that which is magnificent in these chapters (xxiv.–xxvii.) is that the redemption is conceived of as radical, spiritual for mankind. So that the end of the history of redemption is bound together with the beginning, which is written upon the first pages of Genesis.

Who this great prophet was, whether Deutero-Isaiah or another, and when he wrote, whether in the exile or later, can never be satisfactorily explained. That which is relatively most probable is the unity of the great anonymous of chaps. xl.–lxvi. with the great anonymous of chaps. xxiv.–xxvii. With this view we have arranged the concluding portion after II. Isaiah of the time of the exile, the end of which we now pass over.

CHAPTER X.

THE PROPHECY OF THE PERIOD OF THE RESTORATION.

§ 45. *Post-Exilic Prophecy in view of the New Temple.*

AS after the first year of the sole rule of Cyrus (537 B.C.) the people gathered together out of their banishment to their native country, it soon appeared that prophecy is not only θεῖον, but ἀνθρώπινον. The divine plan of salvation is served, not only through the far-sightedness which is rendered possible through the Spirit, but also through the short-sightedness which is not removed; for, if prophecy afforded a chronological knowledge concerning the course of the future, it would render faith, hope, and effort lame, and would aid fleshly security. It is not strange therefore that the prophets of the exile beheld the final glory in close contact with the end of the exile, and that those who returned hoped to live long enough to experience this glory, or at least something of it. But as, in the year 534 B.C., the foundation of the new temple was laid there was mingled with the cry of joy loud weeping over the smallness of the present (Ezra iii. 12 f.), and as under Cambyses the hostility of the Samaritans put a stop to the building of the temple, the people came to experience their ever-enduring servile dependence. Nevertheless, the building of the temple was continued. Darius Hystaspis approved in 520 B.C. the continuation. But those who were building the temple and the city needed such imposing task-masters as Zerubbabel and Joshua, as Ezra, and later Nehemiah ; above all, such prophetic exhorters as Haggai and Zechariah.

The four addresses of the writing of Haggai are all dated after the months and days of the second year of Darius Hystaspis (520 B.C.) of the year of the resumption of the building of the temple. It was given to this prophet to announce that the fulfilling of redemption was connected with the second temple, and the world rule of the house of David with the family of Zerubbabel (cf. Jer. xxii. 24, 30): "Yet once more [is the announcement of God, Hagg. ii. 6–9], it is only a little while until I will shake the heavens, and the earth, the sea, and the mainland, and will shake the nations." From this shaking the temple, as the celebrated centre of the world, will go forth: "and the desirable things of all nations shall come, and I will fill this house with glory, saith Yahweh of hosts." It is shown that here חֶמְדַּת כָּל הַגּוֹיִם is not intended personally of the Messiah, not only from the plural of the predicate בָּאוּ, but also from the following establishment of that which is placed in prospect: " Mine is the silver and mine the gold, utterance of Yahweh of hosts." Under poor circumstances arises now a new temple from the ruins of the old; but He, whose house it is, is the one who possesses all things, and who has all power, who knows how to provide for the adornment of His house (cf. Isa. lx. 5-7). But not only outwardly will this invisible temple be more glorious than the first, but also historically : "Greater shall be the final glory of this house than that in the beginning, saith Yahweh of hosts; and in this place will I give peace—utterance of Yahweh of hosts." Although the wealth of redemption is named here without the mediator of redemption, nevertheless this promise is not to be thought of without relation to the Messiah, who in Isa. ix. 5 f. is called the Prince of peace, whose dominion is directed to peace without end, and concerning whom Micah says (v. 4) that He is שָׁלוֹם, the incarnate peace. Indirectly therefore Haggai prophesies the appearance of the Messiah at the time of the second temple; and since the Herodian rebuilding of the temple was never considered as a third house, בית שלישי, and the temple of Ezekiel must remain out of consideration as a problematical ideal of the future, the Jewish people had reason to expect the Messiah while the post-exilic temple was still standing, and from its destruction in the year 70 A.D. there was the conclusion for those who were unprejudiced, that He must have come already.

The appearance of the Messiah at the time of the second temple was directly prophesied by Zechariah, who entered upon his ministry only two months later than Haggai, in the same second year of Darius (520 B.C.). In the first part of the book which bears his name the Messiah is twice predicted as the future Zemach (צֶמַח), since in chap. iii. as well as in chap.

vi. the present of the prophecy itself is stamped as type of the man of the future. Joshua the high priest and the priests who are subordinate to him are called אַנְשֵׁי מוֹפֵת, *homines prodigii*, which is equivalent to *porridigii*, as such who prepare the way, represent beforehand, and stand security for the coming of the future One; "for behold [thus it is established, iii. 8*b*] I bring hither my servant Zemach." Two things impress themselves even here upon us: (1) this immediate appearance of the Messianic name צֶמַח presupposes the preparation which we find in Isa. iv. 2; Jer. xxiii. 5, xxxiii. 15; (2) while, according to Jeremiah, Zemach (צֶמַח) signifies sprout, which Yahweh causes to sprout to David, hence a Davidic king, which corresponds here to the idea of the kingdom of promise, the priestly side of the future One, is turned forward, for only thus can it be explained that the priesthood which again receives its office is indicated as a prefiguration of the future One. The promise is more extended in vi. 10 ff., where the prophet is enjoined to place a manifold crown (עֲטָרוֹת) upon the head of Joshua the high priest,[1] prepared from the silver and gold provided by the exiles. The words which are directed to Joshua (Zech. vi. 12, 13) indicate what the manifold crown upon one head signifies: "Behold a man whose name is Zemach; and

[1] The modern improvement of text introduces at this point, "and upon the head of Zerubbabel," under the supposition that these words have fallen out from the text. They are rather contrary to it.

from the ground [מִתַּחְתָּיו, from beneath, where he is at home] he shall spring up, and build the temple of Yahweh; yea, he shall build the temple of Yahweh; and he shall receive majesty, and sit and rule upon his throne: and a treaty of peace shall be between them both," namely, between the king and priest, whose dignity and offices he unites in one person. The antagonism, the rivalry of both offices, will be reconciled and removed in his person—the king who is priest for ever after the order of Melchizedek (Ps. cx. 4). And what kind of a temple is that which he shall build? This temple, which is distinguished from the one which is now rising again from the ruins of that of Solomon, cannot possibly be like this—a building of stones. It must be the spiritual temple from living stones (1 Pet. ii. 5) which is intended, in which the promise given to the seed of David, הוּא יִבְנֶה־בַיִת לִשְׁמִי (2 Sam. vii. 13), reaches its ultimate goal.

§ 46. *The Two Christological Pairs of Prophecy in Deutero-Zechariah.*

I. THE FIRST PROPHETIC PAIR IN CHAPS. IX.–XI.

In the brilliant epoch of Old Testament criticism which terminates with the departure of Ewald (May 1875), it was considered just as much proved that Zech. ix.–xiv. belonged to the time before the exile, as that Isa. xl.–lxvi. belonged to the time of the exile itself. In fact, the character of this second part of the Book of Zechariah is so distinguished from the first in matter and language, that adequate grounds for unity of authorship cannot be produced. But it is all the more certain that the author, if he is also not the Zechariah the son of Berechiah, cannot be a pre-exilic prophet, for the Christological images move in the path in which prophecy was directed by Deutero-Isaiah: the δόξαι of the future Christ are supplemented through his preceding παθήματα (1 Pet. i. 11). The two מַשָּׂא out of which this second part consists (ix.–xi., xii.–xiv.) are similar throughout, of the same apocalyptic character as Isa. xxiv.–xxvii. That which is apparently pre-exilic is to be judged in like manner as that which apparently belongs to the Assyrian period: the prophet takes from pre-exilic relations emblematic features for his eschatological pictures. The first prophetic pair in chaps. ix.–xi. treats of the entrance of the king with the air of a sufferer into Jerusalem, and concerning the good shepherd who was rewarded with contempt.

1. The prophet begins in chap. ix. with the prediction concerning the judgments which are visited upon the peoples round about Judah. In the midst of this judgment Zion-Jerusalem is not only shielded, but it becomes the seat of a kingdom ruling the world in peace, ix. 9: "Rejoice greatly, daughter of Zion, exult, daughter of Jerusalem! Behold, thy king comes to thee, righteous, and one whom salvation befalls, poor and riding upon an ass, and upon a foal, the young of an ass." The king who enters for the benefit of Jerusalem, whom it shall greet with jubila-

tion, is צַדִּיק וְנוֹשָׁע a righteous one (cf. Jeremiah's צֶמַח צַדִּיק), and such an one as God has helped out of affliction and struggle to redemption and victory. He has gone through a school of suffering, and is called as נוֹשָׁע also עָנִי. We see him still as a sufferer; the humiliation is not yet transformed into pure and full glory. He does not come mounted on a horse, for he is a king, not as the kings of this world, but a king of a gentle heart and peaceful end (ix. 10*b*): "He speaks peace to the nations, and his government reaches from sea to sea, and from the river to the ends of the earth" (cf. Ps. lxxii. 8).

2. In chap. xi. the prophet receives the command to take the herd of slaughter of the people of God, which is slaughtered and slavishly handled by their own proprietor, under his protection. A time of anarchy, of despotism, of the love of destruction enters. With such prospects and under such circumstances, the poor flock needs more than ever a shepherd. The prophet accomplishes the commission. The symbolical act thus becomes at the same time a vision, the prophet becomes an image of the future One. He feeds the flock of slaughter, and likewise the poor of the flock, devoting to these especially his care. He feeds them with two rods, one of which is called grace (נֹעַם) and the other unity (חֹבְלִים), and removes from the people three shepherds in one month. The three shepherds, as we consider most probable, after the example of Ephrem, Theodoret, and Cyrill, are the three leading orders, since each one is

put forth as a representative of the class of evil prophets, priests, and princes. With this interpretation it is not necessary to understand וָאַכְחִד of the destruction of persons; a destruction is meant which deprives the three kinds of officials of their activity. If the prophet in this symbolical action is a representative of the future Christ, we may understand that he, the prophet, priest, and king in one person, makes room through the removal of the three kinds of bad shepherds. But the kindness which he therewith showed the people was not recognised as it deserved, so that he was weary of his activity. The rejection of the shepherd appointed by God is a rejection of Yahweh Himself, and is avenged in this way, that the people, who were hitherto shielded by God's favour, are made a prize for the attack of the nations of the world. After they compelled him to break the staff of favour, he seeks to lead them to an announcement, by which it shall appear whether they will entirely break off the relation to him as their shepherd or not (xi. 12): "Then I said to them, If it is pleasing to you, give me my reward; but if not, let it go. Then they counted me out as reward thirty pieces of silver." The thirty pieces of silver are a shamefully small valuation of his service, which remind us of the appraisement of a slave (Ex. xxi. 32). "Then Yahweh said to me, Cast it to the potter: the valuable price of which I was considered worth on your part. Then I took the thirty pieces of silver, and cast them to the potter in the house of Yahweh." He is to cast the trifling piece to the potter, so that it may fall into the clay which he kneads, in order that it may be soft and supple,—to the potter in the house of Yahweh, hence in the presence of Yahweh, in order that in this way he may call the people to account for their unthankfulness.[1] Now the good shepherd breaks the staff of unity, and internal disruption comes as a second decree of punishment to the complications with the world-empire. The pre-exile enmity between the kingdoms of Judah and Israel is here and further on only an emblem of a deep rupture which shall divide the Jewish people into halves, one holding to the good shepherd and turning the back to him, hence one that is hostile to Christ, and one that believes in Christ. The prophet now has further (xi. 15–17) to put on the garments of a foolish mad shepherd (רֹעֶה אֱוִלִי), for such an one will oppress the people; nevertheless the judgment of Yahweh falls upon him: "Woe to the shepherd of negation [*Verneinung*, רֹעִי הָאֱלִיל, with *i* as a connective sound] who forsakes the flock! Sword over his arm, and over his right

---

[1] With the casting [of the thirty pieces of silver] into the clay of the potter there is easily connected the thought, that the people, who thus reward the good shepherd, require a transformation. Thus is to be explained the proof in the history of fulfilment (Matt. xxvii. 9 f.) that the thirty pieces of silver, the price of treachery, for the purchase of the potter's field, *i.e.* of such an one who dealt in clay, was applied, and at the same time how the remembrance of the one citing could fall upon Jer. xviii. 4: "And if the vessel displeased him which he made, he made it into another vessel, just as it was pleasing to the potter to do.'

eye! his arm shall be entirely dried up, and his right eye entirely extinguished." Both מַשָּׂא delight in such shocking pictures. If the good shepherd is the future Christ, the foolish shepherd, whose character and ministry stand related to those of a shepherd as " no " to " yes " (cf. Job xiii. 4), is the Antichrist. The retrogressive movement of that which is prophesied is common also to both מַשָּׂא. The two prophetic images in chaps. ix. and xi. are a hysteron proteron ; for first the future One consumes himself in work for his people, and then he is raised from lowliness to a kingdom which rules the world.

§ 47. *The Two Christological Pairs of Prophecy in Deutero-Zechariah.*

II. THE SECOND PROPHETIC PAIR IN CHAPS. XII.–XIV.

The first מַשָּׂא began as the sound of judgment on the nations in Amos, and the second as the judgment on the nations in the valley of Jehoshaphat, according to Joel. We meet in chap. xii., in the universal battle of the peoples which is described against Yahwism, Judah itself among the enemies who are laying siege to Jerusalem. It is exclusively Deutero-Zechariah in whom the division of Israel against itself is formed to such an eschatological picture. Judah makes common cause with the world, which is hostile to the God of salvation ; but in the midst of the climax of its enmity he comes to his senses, and does what he can to free Jerusalem, since the light which has risen upon him has become a consuming fire to all who are opposed to it. Judah has passed to the side of the world, but will be brought around, and will be still earlier free from the bonds of the hostile world than Jerusalem itself, which goes forth from this danger of destruction more firmly and gloriously than ever: "On that day Yahweh will shield the inhabitants of Jerusalem; and the one who stumbles among them on that day shall be as David; and the house of David as Elohim, as the angel of Yahweh before them." In xii. 10 ff. the prophet establishes that which he presupposes (ver. 2), that there will be a Jerusalem true to God and beloved by God at a time when Judah finds himself on the side of the enemy: "And I will pour out upon the house of David, and upon the inhabitants of Jerusalem, the spirit of grace and of supplication for grace; and they shall look to me [the Massoretic reading אֵלַי is confirmed by the LXX., the Targum, the Peshitto, and Jerome] whom they have pierced, and they shall lament for him, like the lamentation for the only one, and shall weep bitterly for him, as one weeps bitterly for his first-born. In that day the lamentation shall be great in Jerusalem, like the lamentation in Hadadrimmon in the valley of Megiddo [that is, like the lamentation for Josiah, the best beloved king, 2 Chron. xxxv. 22—25]. And the land shall wail, all the families apart; the family of David apart, and their wives apart; the family of Nathan apart, and their wives apart [that is, the royal house of the line of Solomon, and of the side line of Nathan]; the family of the house of Levi apart, and their wives apart; the family of Shimei apart, and their wives apart [that is, the house of Levi of the main lines Gershon, Kohath, and Merari, and the side line of Shimei, Num. iii. 21]; all the families that remain preserved, every family apart, and their wives apart."

Since, now, the Spirit from above drives the people of Jerusalem into the pain of penitence to this extent, yet in the realization of its guilt of sin it does not need to be in despair (xiii. 1): "On that day there shall be a fountain opened to the house of David, and to the inhabitants of Jerusalem, for sin and uncleanness" [that is, a fountain of living water, which washes away sin and pollution].

Who is the great pierced One, in whom Yahweh sees Himself as pierced, as hurt? In spite of the fact that the New Testament Scriptures explain that Christ is this pierced One, modern exegesis places a stranger, concerning whom we know nothing, hence an x in the place of Christ. But it can only be the מְחֹלָל of Isaiah (liii. 1)—hence the servant of Yahweh, or, as we could also say, since the lamentation for him is compared with the lamentation for Josiah, the king Messiah. The great national repentance on account of the murder of him with whom Yahweh was so personally connected, that he identified Himself with him, has, indeed, its like exclusively only in the sorrowful repentant confession with which Israel of the final period (Isa. liii.), ashamed of its blindness, recognises its national guilt.

After the prophetic picture of repentance for the recognised guilt of bloodshed, there now follows, after the peculiar manner of this Deutero-Zechariah, in the movement from that which is farther to that which is nearer, the prophetic image of the shepherd beloved by God who is smitten by the sword of Yahweh (xiii. 7): "Sword, rise against my Shepherd, and against the man of my alliance—utterance of Yahweh of hosts; smite the Shepherd, so that the sheep may be scattered; and I will turn my hand to the little ones." If we are right when we compare the great repentance (Zech. xii.) with the great confession (Isa. liii.), by the same analogy we may compare Zech. xiii. 7 with Isa. liii. 10: "It pleased Yahweh to crush him; he hath caused Him pain." He willed the end, the reconciliation, and hence also the means, the vicarious death of His servant. This is the good shepherd who was paid off with thirty pieces of silver; this is the One also whom Yahweh's sword smites, while he yet stands in the closest fellowship with Him. Sword indicates here in general, as in Ps. xxii. 11, the instrument of murder. Yahweh Himself summons the sword, for all the sins of men unintentionally serve God's plan, and, especially, in this judicial murder God's decree was subserved. From the blood-guiltiness there grows up for the people who were guilty of it misfortune, for which they were responsible: the death of the shepherd had as its result the scattering of the flock. But there are such from whom God's grace does not turn away, those who are lightly esteemed, and who think little of themselves, whose feeling is not that of the mass.

These are the two prophetic pairs of Deutero-Zechariah, in which the *ecce-homo* form of the Christ, which forms the mighty foundation of His royal glory, comes in striking small pictures to representation. In the pre-exilic period these prophecies could not be introduced into the course of development, but now they are the fruit of the new formation of the Messianic hope which appears in Isa. xl.–lxvi.

§. 48. *Concluding Prophecies of New Testament Contents in Malachi.*

Deutero-Zechariah prophesies concerning the good shepherd, but the aim of the history of redemption is expressed in Zech. xiv. 9 : " Yahweh one, and His name one ; " but not yet, as afterwards when the Good Shepherd appeared bodily: "one fold, one shepherd" (John x. 16). When in chap. xiv. he causes all peoples to make a pilgrimage to Jerusalem, in order to celebrate there with the people of God the feast of Tabernacles, this loveliest, most familiar, most joyous, and best adapted for uniting men in brotherhood of the Israelitish national festivals, this is not a plunging into Jewish ceremonial legality, but only a development of a thought already expressed in the old prophetic word (Isa. ii. 2 f.; Micah iv. 1 f.), which also Deutero-Isaiah develops. For him also in chap. lx. Jerusalem is the point in the east from which the

sun of the completed kingdom of God arises. Both of the great prophets, whose image of the Messiah is so true to the New Testament, do not yet follow out the removal of the wall of partition between Israel and the nations to its New Testament consequences. But if, now, one of the three post-exilic prophets decentralizes the worship of Yahweh, so that he also recognises outside of Jerusalem a worship of Yahweh, which is well-pleasing. in the presentation of offerings, we must hold that this prophet, from the standpoint of prophetic history, is the last of the three; for the knowledge which he affords goes beyond the prophets of the exile. But this is true of Malachi, whom we may not even for this reason place before Ezra, and, indeed, before 444 B.C. (the reading of the law, Neh. viii. 1–12), as is done on insufficient grounds of Pentateuch criticism by Reuss, Giesebrecht, and others; but above all we may not place him before Ezra, because the public circumstances, with whose censure he has to do, are the same as those found by Nehemiah in his second residence in Jerusalem after 412 B.C.; for example, the immorality of mixed marriages which prevailed again (Neh. xiii. 23 ; cf. Mal. ii. 11 f., and with it Deut. xxiii. 4–6). His reproof in i. 6–ii. 6 is directed against the priests. Yahweh had no pleasure in the priests as they were at that time: He was not willing to accept the meal-offerings which they brought (מִנְחָה, by synechdoche, embraces the other offerings, i. 11):
"For from the rising of the sun to its going down my name is great among the heathen, and in all

places incense is burned, and sacrifices are made to my name, and, indeed [וּ, *epexegeticum*], a pure meal-offering: for great is my name among the heathen, saith Yahweh of hosts." It is scarcely possible that the prophet says this concerning the heathen world of the present; the expression would go much further over that, which can be accepted as the working of preparatory grace in the heathen world, namely, as Deutero-Isaiah (xlii. 4) says: an unconscious waiting for the torah of the servant of Yahweh, joined with the feeling of the need of redemption. It is therefore that which is future which Malachi expresses as present. But however we may interpret it, it certainly is involved in the words בַּגּוֹיִם וּבְכָל מָקוֹם that the sacrificial torah will cease to be exclusively bound to Jerusalem. The prophet expresses in Old Testament form the same which Jesus answered to the question of the Samaritan woman (John iv. 23). Even this one prophetic word makes Malachi one of the greatest prophets. It is at the same time significant that the sacrifice which the peoples bring Yahweh, with an aversion to the bloody animal sacrifices, are designated as מִנְחָה טְהוֹרָה, that is, as a pure meal-offering (see Isa. lxvi. 20): that is also a step forward to the New Testament worship of God "in spirit and in truth" (ἐν πνεύματι καὶ ἀληθείᾳ). Malachi reproves another cancerous affection of the people from ii. 17 on to the end of this book. Led by the blasphemous language of those who miss in the present course of the world the righteous distribution of happiness and misery, he prophesies a day of Yahweh which shall reveal the difference between the godless and those who fear God. They ask (ii. 17): "Where is the God of judgment?" The answer of God through His prophets is as follows (iii. 1): "Behold, I send my angel, and he prepares the way before me; and suddenly shall come to his temple the Lord [הָאָדוֹן] whom ye seek [here the distinctive accent *rebîa*]; and the angel of the covenant whom ye desire: behold, he comes, saith Yahweh of hosts." That which follows is description of the judgment. The Lord, that is, Yahweh, comes and holds judgment over the degenerate priesthood [the children of Levi], and the mass of the people who are sunken in vice; and from this smelting of judgment a priesthood goes forth that is pleasing to God, and a congregation of righteous people: those who fear God, who had previously vanished in the mass, and who are trodden down, attain dominion. The angel who prepares the way for the Lord is, according to ver. 23 f., Elijah the prophet, who appears as a preacher of repentance to turn the hearts of the fathers to the children, and the hearts of the children to their fathers, that is, in order to make up for the contrast between the present and the better past, in order that the judgment might not be a work of annihilation. On the contrary, the mention of the angel of the covenant (מַלְאַךְ הַבְּרִית) in ver. 1*b* remains isolated; the work of the future appears from ver. 2 forward as a work of Yahweh Himself. This is elsewhere true in the prophets, with their deepest, most

NEW TESTAMENT IN MALACHI.

Christological words; they are only more or less like lightning which flashes through the darkness. Everything in chap. iii. is deeply significant. Even the prediction of the angel who precedes the Lord takes on a form after the words of the torah, which speak of מַלְאַךְ ה׳ (Ex. xxiii. 20, xxxiii. 2; cf. the form of the citation, Matt xi. 10), and not only in form, but also in fact. מַלְאַךְ הַבְּרִית refers back to the angelophanies of the patriarchal history, which, according to the conclusion of the covenant (Gen. xv. with Gen. xvi.), are related mediately to the actualization of the promises of the covenant. The word מַלְאָךְ signifies in Mal. ii. 7 a messenger sent by God. מַלְאַךְ הַבְּרִית, hence a messenger of God, who mediates a new covenant between God and His people. And since this mediator of the covenant in the parallel halves of the verse stands on the same basis with the Lord Himself, the prophet must think of the Lord as coming in this מַלְאַךְ הַבְּרִית and the thought suggests itself that the punitive historical appearance of Yahweh in His angel finds therein its antitype. The prophet connects the Lord and this angel of the covenant so closely together that he ascribes to those who wish for the coming of God as judge at the same time the coming of this מַלְאָךְ, because the desire for the one involves in it the unintentional desire for the other.

§ 49. *The Antichrist in the Book of Daniel.*

We now turn for the first time to the Book of Daniel, since this book, as it lies before us, was only written about the year 168 B.C., and therefore still found admission, when the canon, which was divided into Torah, Nebiim, and Kethûbîm, was already in existence. Daniel, with his three friends, belongs to the servants of Yahweh among the exiles who mourned for Zion, and who were ready to seal their faith with the surrender of their lives. The historicity of his person is vouched for by Ezekiel, who mentions him (xiv. 14, 20) as a pre-eminent צַדִּיק, and (xxviii. 3) as a pre-eminent חָכָם, with a tendency to the mysterious. But the book which bears his name does not claim to have been written by him. As Isa. xl.–lxvi. is a book of comfort for the Babylonian exiles, the Book of Daniel is a book of comfort for the confessors and martyrs of the time of the Seleucidae. It digests traditional Babylonio-Persian histories and traditional predictions of Daniel as examples of fidelity in the faith, and promises of delivery from great tribulation. The post-exilic origin of the book is also favoured through its doctrinal contents. As in the vision of Zechariah of the four spans (vi. 1–8), the four world-powers, represented through the spotted strong horses, in the course of the vision are divided into two, the spotted horses, an image of the empire of Alexander, joined together through the union of the Orient and Occident, and the strong horses are an image of the Roman Empire; so the fourth world-empire in the Book of Daniel is the Grecian, behind which, however, the Roman also appears. The enigmatic words of Balaam (Num. xxiv. 24) with reference to a Western world-power find here their explanation. Even in Deutero-Zechariah (ix. 13), Zion and Javan, as the kingdom of God and the kingdom of the world, are contrasted. The Book of Daniel, however, has the conflict of the Jewish religion against the heathen Grecian religion as its main object. And here for the first time there comes to a detailed representation what had previously only been hinted at (Ps. lxviii. 22, cx. 6; Isa. xi. 9; Hab. iii 13; Zech. xi. 15–17), that the enmity of the world against the Church and its God should finally be combined in the person of a single individual, and would extend to a mortal struggle with the Church. Antiochus Epiphanes seeks to do away with the Jewish religion and the exclusive Jewish nationality at any price. The utmost tribulation continues for the period of half a Sabbath, hence three and a half years. But the climax of the tribulation is the turn to redemption. Thus the book prophesies, and thus it really came to pass. Before the conclusion of the year 165 B.C., the temple, which had been profaned through the $\beta\theta\acute{\epsilon}\lambda\upsilon\gamma\mu\alpha$ $\grave{\epsilon}\rho\eta\mu\acute{\omega}\sigma\epsilon\omega\varsigma$, was again consecrated, and Antiochus atoned for a plundering expedition against Elymais with his life. The Book of Daniel has in its images and predictions an apocalyptic character; the prediction of future events goes back to those which are past, and takes these, in that which is related in a prophetic way, as predetermined antecedents; whether xi. 30 is a pure prediction, fulfilled through the appearance of the Roman fleet before Alexandria with the ambassador C. Popilius Laenas, who compelled Antiochus to vacate Egypt, and [through] the restoration of Ptolemaeus Philometor, 168 B.C., can remain undetermined; but the rescue from the persecution which began at that time, and from the violent transformation of the temple of Yahweh into a temple of Zeus Olympios (167 B.C.), must be prophecy, since the book is made without a purpose when that which is prophesied in xi. 31 ff. is degraded to a prophecy after the event. The book must have been written before the liberation of the fearfully persecuted people from their arch-enemy Antiochus Epiphanes. It does not know any other antichrist except him; but the progress of the history has shown that not only Antiochus, but also Nero, are only forerunners, prototypes of the final Antichrist.

§ 50. *Christ in the Book of Daniel.*

Luther, in the vision of the seventy weeks (ix. 25 f.), translates twice—and exclusively only these two passages—מָשִׁיחַ as Christus: sixty-nine weeks until "Christ the Prince," and "after sixty weeks Christ shall be destroyed, and shall be no more." But if, as without doubt is right, the parousia of Christ the Prince, Hebrew מָשִׁיחַ נָגִיד, falls in the seventy weeks, the מָשִׁיחַ who is destroyed cannot also be the Christ. The connection מָשִׁיחַ נָגִיד is favourable to the view that מָשִׁיחַ has not the signification of the anointed king, but of the anointed priest. And since the future view of Daniel has this in common with every prophetic view of the future, that with the end of the present time of tribulation it beholds the final period, nothing is more probable than that the מָשִׁיחַ who shall be destroyed is the high priest Onias III., after whose removal (176 B.C.) Antiochus plundered the temple and massacred 40,000 Jews; and that מָשִׁיחַ נָגִיד, in distinction from מָשִׁיחַ, the high priest, and נָגִיד, the world ruler (26b), indicates the one who is מָשִׁיחַ and נָגִיד, or, as Zechariah (vi. 13) prophesied, is כֹּהֵן and מוֹשֵׁל, priest and king in one person. On the contrary, the stone which breaks in pieces the image of marble (ii. 44) is referred to the everlasting kingdom of the final period, and also in the explanation of the one who, like the Son of man (כְּבַר אֱנָשׁ), is brought on the clouds of heaven before the Ancient of Days (that is, God who is eternal, with reference to the past as well as the future), who gives him the everlasting rule over the world, only the עַם קַדִּישֵׁי עֶלְיוֹנִין is thought of, not expressly the one who as the one who appeared with reference to it named himself ὁ υἱὸς τοῦ ἀνθρώπου. But in ix. 25 the Messiah appears from the Messianic people as priestly king. And if this is found disputable, yet it remained indisputable that even the description of the future salvation makes the Book of Daniel worthy to have the last word in the Old Testament canon: 'Seventy weeks are determined upon thy people and upon thy city to put a stop to crime, to cause sin to cease, and to atone for evil-doing; and to create an everlasting righteousness, and to seal [namely, through fulfilment] vision and prophecy, and to anoint that which is most holy." Here the aim of Old Testament hope is spiritually apprehended and expressed with almost dogmatic clearness.